Who's Afraid of the Old Testament God?

ALDEN THOMPSON

Academie
Books Grand Rapids, Michigan
Zondervan Publishing House

Who's Afraid
— of the —
Old Testament
God?

Who's Afraid of the Old Testament God?
Copyright © 1989 by Alden Thompson
First published in 1988. This edition published by special
arrangement with The Paternoster Press

ACADEMIE BOOKS is an imprint of Zondervan Publishing House,
1415 Lake Drive, S.E., Grand Rapids, Michigan 49506.

Library of Congress Cataloging in Publication Data

Thompson, Alden L. (Alden Lloyd)
    Who's afraid of the Old Testament God? / Alden Thompson.
        p.   cm.
    ISBN 0-310-51921-7
    1. God–Biblical teaching.   2. Bible.   O.T.-
-Criticism, interpretation, etc.   3. Bible.   N.T.–Relation to the
Old Testament.   I. Title.
    BS1192.6T48   1989
    231–dc20   89-39730
                                                                                    CIP

Printed in the United States of America

89 90 91 92 93 94 / PP / 10 9 8 7 6 5 4 3 2 1

Dedicated
to my gentle wife
WANDA
who still does not enjoy
reading the Old Testament
—in spite of all my urgings
and explanations

Contents

Preface

For some time this book has been threatening to find its way onto paper. The urging of friends, the needs of the college classroom, and my concern for the life of the Christian community, are all significant arguments as to why the task should have been completed long before now. Every chapter contains material that has proved to be a real blessing in my own Christian experience. In the end, the urge to share that experience provided the motivation that has finally brought the work to completion.

I write as a conservative Christian with a deep concern for the life of the conservative Christian community. My hope is that the book will appeal both to those who have been part of such a community all their lives, and to those who find themselves attracted for one reason or another to the kind of life and experience offered by a conservative approach to the Christian tradition.

On the basis of my own observations, I am convinced that within this approach to Christianity lies great potential for good or for evil. The strong religious convictions which are generally a part of conservative Christianity can lead to a beautiful and liberating experience, but gone awry, can result in bitterness, hostility, or despair. Ultimately, whether our experience blossoms or withers depends on the kind of God we serve and the kind of God we find revealed through Scripture.

You may find it surprising that it was actually the Old Testament that brought my Christian experience to life. The Old Testament God generally has a rather poor reputation, even in Christian circles. But it was indeed my study of the Old Testament which has forced me to re-examine my understanding of God and has led me to a

much clearer grasp of how he would have me live and
what he would have me believe about him.

Throughout the book you will recognize an active dialogue with the New Testament, with traditional Christian
positions, with modern scholarship and with Christian experience. The book is not really designed to be 'scholarly',
but it does attempt to show how modern scholarship can
often shed fresh light on biblical interpretation. I have
discovered that taking a fresh look at Scripture in the light
of modern scholarship can lead to very worthwhile gains
in the understanding of Scripture, and thus for Christian
experience.

Conservatives have often been quite hostile to modern
scholarship; part of the reason for that hostility no doubt
stems from the rough treatment that their approach has
sometimes received at the hands of biblical scholars. In
any event, more heat than light has often been generated,
and that has been most unfortunate. My own serious
exposure to modern biblical scholarship came from the
faculty of New College at the University of Edinburgh,
under the direction of men who were extremely helpful
even though they did not always share my convictions.
They asked the questions that I needed to face, questions
that conservatives have often avoided. The experience
forced me to confront God and his word in a way that
ultimately has led to this book.

Fundamental to the approach I have taken is the position that 'All Scripture is inspired by God' (2 Tim. 3:16).
That means Old Testament as well as New. Furthermore, I
am convinced that we should never let Christian tradition
or even another passage of Scripture rob us of the opportunity of coming afresh to each passage of Scripture as
God's word to us. The Bible is normative, but we must not
impose upon it a false unity which would have the practical effect of denying canonical status to certain parts of
Scripture. Conservatives have often overlooked that
canonical principle, if not in theory, at least in practice, for
we have often assumed that the New Testament must
always have the last word even in the interpretation of
Old Testament passages. I develop this argument in the

first chapter, probably the most crucial one in the book, though others may be more helpful in other ways.

The discovery that I want to share above all else is that the Scriptures of the Old Testament can remain alive and can lead us to a fresh appreciation of all that God has done for us. That really is what the gospel is all about.

CHAPTER ONE

Don't let your New Testament get in the way of your Old Testament

In many and various ways God spoke of old . . .
in these last days he has spoken to us by a Son
(Hebrews 1:1–2).

'Some day I am going to write a book about all the unchristian sayings in the New Testament!' Thus, in a tone at least partially serious, a well-known Old Testament scholar revealed his unhappiness with the sometimes less-than-subtle claim of his New Testament colleagues that theirs was the superior Testament. According to the common generalization, the New Testament is the source of all that is good, kind, and loving, embodied most of all in the person of Jesus Christ who reveals the friendly face of God. As the story goes, however, the Old Testament is at best a mixed bag. The occasional flash of brilliance may lighten the path of the believer, but on the whole, the angry, the vindictive, the bloodthirsty, is far more prominent.

Now I suspect that there is at least a grain of truth in this common view of the two parts of our Christian Bible. At least I have never heard a Christian contrast the beauty and attractiveness of the Old Testament with the horrors of the New. No, Christians have always found refuge in the New Testament when the problems of the Old Testament have threatened to engulf them. In fact, some Christians even go so far as to claim with emphasis that they are *New Testament* Christians for whom the Old Testament is no longer authoritative.

Even if the problems with the Old Testament should stem from some monumental misunderstanding, the fact that such a misunderstanding is so common is something we must reckon with. But perhaps at the outset I should remind you of some of the likely candidates for my friend's book on the so-called unchristian aspects of the New Testament. Wasn't it Jesus who suggested that certain people deserved to have a millstone fastened round their necks and to be drowned in the depths of the sea (Matt. 18:6)? And didn't he openly call some people blind hypocrites, comparing them to an old burial ground, full of dead men's bones (Matt. 23:27–28)? And then there was Peter. For all practical purposes he told Ananias and Sapphira to drop dead (Acts 5:1–11). To add to the stories, Paul told the church at Corinth to deliver one of their brothers to Satan for the destruction of the flesh (1 Cor. 5:5), and to drive out the wicked person from among them (1 Cor. 5:13). Finally, we must not forget the book of Revelation: blood, dragons, pits of fire, and even a God who spews people out of his mouth (Rev. 3:16).

You could rightly accuse me of greatly distorting the faith by bringing that particular collection of sayings and events together without regard for context or the author's apparent intention. But that is precisely what happens to the Old Testament. Having grown up in the Christian community, I know the basic Old Testament 'list' quite well. Pride of place goes to poor Uzzah who was only trying to be helpful when stumbling oxen endangered the ark of God, yet God struck him dead (2 Sam. 6:6–9); two angry bears mauled forty-two 'innocent' children who were disrespectful to their elders (2 Kings 2:23–25). If you are so bold as to complain about the way God is doing things, then he will send serpents to bite you (Num. 21:4–9) or he will command the earth to swallow you alive (Num. 16:21–35). If you wish, you may add to the list the Genesis flood and the burning of Sodom and Gomorrah, for these, too, have often been cited as part of the evidence for a heavy-handed Old Testament God who flies into a destructive range the moment someone crosses his will or breaks one of his commands.

Now I hope that you will pardon the way in which I have listed the above horror stories. If it is not already too late, I should perhaps even make a special plea right here for you *not* to toss aside such an irreverent book as this. I have several good friends who think it highly inappropriate ever to say anything that even hints at the slightest deficiency in God's style of leadership (perhaps taking their cue from Romans 9:20), and they are quick to caution me about the dangers of doubt. I am sensitive to those who feel that way, for I, too, am deeply concerned about the damage that doubt can cause. In this world, none of us is ever 'safe' from doubt, but as I put these words on paper, I must say that my convictions about the goodness of God are deeper and stronger because I have looked squarely at my 'small' doubts and have found answers which have brought genuine blessing.

When I say 'small' doubts, I am alluding to the fact that my experience has always been within the Christian community. I am the product of a careful and devout Christian home—a home for which I am immensely thankful. At the same time, the Old Testament stories (and the New Testament ones) of the type listed above can leave scars when mishandled and applied wrongly, even by well-meaning Christians. I know that I am not alone in having had at least 'small' doubts as a result of biblical material misunderstood and misapplied. Small doubts can easily mushroom into large ones and become extremely destructive. Indeed, even small doubts are no fun. But what is perhaps most significant for this book is that the very material which previously had been the cause of doubt has now become the source of great blessing.

So I intend to speak quite frankly about some of the 'problems' of the Old Testament. I really hope that those who have struggled with these same problems will also be able to transform their doubts into cornerstones of faith. From my own experience, I am convinced that once we have found faith, we must resist the attempt to command it in others. My doubts have seldom if ever yielded to mere commands, least of all to commands not to doubt! I must take my problems seriously. To be able to believe is a precious possession, one that I covet for all of God's children. And though I am sure that no two of us ever find precisely the same path to faith, I am going to approach the problems directly, assuming that those insights that have been a great help to me can also be of help to someone else.

A 'BETTER' REVELATION?

Right at the beginning of this chapter I noted the sharp contrast that is often drawn between the Old Testament and the New. That contrast is very important and we must not simply deny that it exists, for the very fact that God has chosen such different ways of revealing himself is part of the truth that he wants us to understand. We need no better authority than the book of Hebrews to remind us, that, in some ways at least, the New Testament revelation of God is, in fact, better. The theme of the entire book is that the revelation of God in Jesus Christ is 'better'. The very first verse reminds us that in times past God used other methods of revealing his will, but now he has spoken through his Son (Heb. 1:1–2). But in chapter twelve the contrast is even more explicit: you have not come to a mountain of smoke, fire, and fear, but to Mt. Zion and to Jesus (Heb. 12:18–24). When I finally realized what those verses were saying, I was startled, for I had grown up in a Christian community which stressed the significance of the Sinai revelation. So in the light of a 'better' revelation (the clear thrust of the book of Hebrews), what are we to do with the older revelation, the one which centres on Sinai?

For a start, the word 'better' can express two rather different emphases. First, 'better' is often simply in contrast with 'worse': yesterday your cold was 'worse'— running eyes, a frightful cough, a hoarse voice—but today it and you are 'better'. If that is the sort of contrast intended in Hebrews between the 'better' Jesus Christ and the 'worse' Mount Sinai, then the God of Sinai is indeed in trouble—as well as anyone who attempts to proclaim that both revelations are part of the Christian faith.

The second way of looking at 'better' is to see it simply as the comparative of 'good'; the revelation at Mount Sinai was good, and the revelation in Jesus Christ was 'better'. Maybe we could even add the superlative: personal reunion with God in his kingdom will be 'best'. If we can take such an approach to the two historical revelations of God, then there is no need to reject the first revelation; rather we may see it as a major step in God's plan of restoring man, and it is a good step at that. In fact, the Sinai revelation was precisely what God's people needed at that time.

One illustration that has helped me to visualize the relationship between 'better' and 'good' has to do with my boyhood experience with the family cars. It fell to my lot to keep the 'buggy', as we affectionately dubbed it, clean and polished. Over the weeks and months I became quite good friends with the car. I knew each scratch and chip and did my best to touch them up or to polish them out. This personal friendship with the car became a problem only when it finally became evident that a new and better car was needed. I well remember when we sold our beloved little 1950 Chevrolet. It had been a good car, even though we had moved on to something better—a 1956 Ford. Thereafter I would occasionally catch a glimpse of the Chev., now under the care of its new owners. A peculiar sensation of excitement and disappointment would strike me: 'There's our old car! Oh, but it's not ours any more!' Perhaps those feelings explain why that next car, the '56 Ford, is still in the family. Its finely polished, deep metallic green is still a sight to warm the heart. Newer and better cars have come and gone, but that old one is still 'good'. It doesn't have air conditioning, something very helpful in the desert regions of the West, and we probably wouldn't take it on a long trip, but it was and is a good car. When we first bought it, it was just what the family needed and even now is a source of warm memories—as well as quite an adequate vehicle for short journeys.

I look on the relationship between Mount Sinai and Jesus Christ in a very similar way. I find the revelation of God in Christ a clearer and better revelation, but I certainly need not deny the marvellous experience that God gave to his people at Mount Sinai. It was just what they needed and it was good. Even today I can relive that experience and be blessed. The fullness of the revelation in Jesus can be joyfully received as Part Two of God's great drama without detracting in the slightest from the marvels of Part One as described in the Old Testament. With any good book it is possible to hasten ahead and read the conclusion without ever bothering with what precedes. If we do that with our Bibles, however, we are missing a real treat and we are letting the New Testament get in the way of the Old. Yes, the New Testament revelation of God is clearer and therefore in some ways better. But if we neglect the Old in favour of the New, we shall never really experience that peculiar kind of joy that comes from experiencing the movement of God's great plan from 'good' to 'better'—and to 'best'.

TWO APPROACHES TO THE OLD TESTAMENT:
THE HIGH ROAD AND THE LOW ROAD

Another way in which the New Testament often gets in the way of the Old is also illustrated by the book of Hebrews. In particular, I am thinking of the famous 'faith' chapter, Hebrews 11. If you read that chapter carefully and compare the stories there with the first accounts told in the Old Testament, you will notice a fascinating tendency in Hebrews to tell the stories in such a way that God's men of ages past are all seen to be great men of faith. Perhaps it would not be too far amiss to compare what is happening in that list of stories to what often takes place at a funeral. Regardless of what kind of life a person has lived, the official memorial service remembers only the good. The deceased may have been a real villain, but you couldn't guess that from what is said in public! Hebrews 11 doesn't contain anything quite that extreme, but certainly the highlights of faith tend to exclude those less than complimentary features of the original Old Testament stories. Let's note just a few examples.

The Genesis picture of Abraham is a man of faith—but one whose convictions often wavered when put to the test. His half-truths to Pharaoh about Sarah showed not only his lack of faith in God, but also his selfishness and lack of genuine respect for his wife (Gen. 12:1–20). Likewise, when he decided that Hagar could bear the child of promise (Gen. 16), he betrayed an uncertain faith. To be sure, these lapses of faith can actually be encouraging to us, for here is a man with serious difficulties yet who was adjudged to be faithful (Heb. 11:8–19). The point that I want to make, however, is that the *original* Old Testament story is essential if one is to reap maximum benefit from the story in Hebrews. Hebrews 11 taken by itself is a fine story, but taken alongside the Old Testament story it becomes superb.

The mention of Sarah and of Moses in Hebrews 11 provides further examples of a partial telling of the Old Testament story. Hebrews 11:11 says that 'by faith' Sarah conceived. Would you have guessed that she actually had laughed when God first made the promise to her—unless of course you had read the Old Testament story (Gen. 18:9–15)? And the contrast in Moses' case is even sharper, for the Exodus story of the killing of the Egyptian and Moses' flight from Pharaoh makes it quite clear that Moses fled because he was afraid (Ex. 2:14). But Hebrews 11:27 says that 'by faith' he left Egypt, 'not (!) being afraid' of the anger of the king. The *apparent* contradiction between the two stories is resolved by a clearer understanding of what 'by faith' means in Hebrews 11, namely, that faith can work wonders even when the human agent does not really appear to be faithful. Yet that particular understanding of faith is possible only when one carefully compares the original Old Testament story with the interpretation of that story in Hebrews 11. Now I happen to believe that both the Old Testament and the New Testament stories have an independent value of their own and should be appreciated for their own sake, but linking the two together enhances our ability to understand God's activities. I shall return to this point later, but now I want to note what has happened to the general interpretation of the Old Testament in view of the treatment that it receives in Hebrews 11.

Just as Hebrews 11 tends to focus on the highlights of Old Testament characters, emphasizing their faithfulness, their godliness, their commitment, so subsequent Christian interpretation has tended to glorify this 'royal line' of God-fearing people. Such an emphasis is valuable; in an age when heroes are hard to come by, it is important to understand what a real hero is. Nevertheless, I remember my surprise when I actually got around to reading the Old Testament stories themselves after having heard only *Christian interpretations* of these stories. Some of the realistic and seamier aspects of the biblical characters came as real surprises. The horrors of polygamy didn't really snap clear until I read the biblical edition of the story of Jacob's family. The book of Esther is even more surprising. I had pictured her as a virtuous young lady without any taint—the feminine counterpart of Daniel. But when I actually read the biblical account, I began to realize that her standards of morality were quite different from mine. Not only was she willing to keep quiet about her convictions (Esther 2:10), but she was willing simply to be one of the girls, a part of the Persian king's harem (Esther 2:12–18)! Daniel stood firmly for his convictions and his standards of morality line up rather well with what a modern Christian would consider appropriate. But Esther . . .!

I began to realize that Christians have often taken a 'high road' approach to the Old Testament, which, in my case at least, had left me quite unprepared for the reading of the Bible itself. Subconsciously I had formed an image of Abraham, Isaac, and Jacob as classic saints who could quite easily slip into twentieth century dress and, if called upon, could easily assume positions of leadership in the Christian community. I suspect that this glorified conception of Old Testament saints is at least part of the reason why many Christians tend to read interpretations and adaptations of the Old Testament instead of actually reading the Old Testament itself. The emphasis on the good qualities of biblical characters is very necessary, especially in the training of younger children, but I feel keenly about the need to prepare Christians for the actual reading of the Old Testament, and to prepare them for coming to grips with the real Old Testament stories, even though many of them are not pretty when viewed strictly from an aesthetic point of view.

I sometimes use the term 'low road' to describe an approach to the Old Testament which takes account of the failings of the biblical characters and their strange, even barbaric, customs. The implications of this 'low road' approach will be pursued further in chapter 2, but the point I wish to make here is, that the 'high road' approach (cf. Hebrews 11), when not accompanied by the 'low road', leaves one quite unprepared for the reading of the Old Testament itself. Thus, when a sensitive person comes upon a story which depicts how far the people had fallen, rather than how far they had grown, the natural reaction is to shy away from the Old Testament and resort to safer reading in the Gospels. In a sense, then, the New Testament has got in the way of the Old.

This predominance of the 'high road' approach in dealing with the Old Testament came rather forcibly to my attention one day in my elementary Hebrew class. The class was composed of upper division ministerial students who were, in most cases, not more than a few months away from entering the ministry. The exercises in our grammar book had been modelled on biblical phrases so as to prepare the students for the reading of the biblical passages, and it was one of these exercises that caused an interesting problem for several members of the class. Correctly translated, one particular exercise should have read: 'And Samuel cut off the head of the king.' Since the Hebrew was not difficult even for first-year students, I asked why this particular sentence had been a problem. Most revealing was the reply volunteered by one of my students: 'We thought that was what the sentence said, but we didn't think that Samuel would do such a thing!' I suggested we take our Bibles and read (in English) the story of Agag in 1 Samuel. To one thoroughly familiar with the Old Testament, the story of Agag might raise certain questions, but the particulars would not be surprising. Yet it was a subdued group of ministerial students who listened in some astonishment to the following words: 'And Samuel said, "As your sword has made women childless, so shall your mother be childless among women." And Samuel hewed Agag in pieces before the Lord in Gilgal' (1 Sam. 15:33).

In the discussion that followed, it became evident that they had been deeply impressed with the 'high road' picture of the innocent and obedient boy Samuel in the temple, saying: 'Speak, for thy servant hears' (1 Sam. 3:10). How could that little boy take a sword and hew a man in pieces—even if it was before the Lord? Such a strange act for such a good lad! To come down to our own age, it would seem even stranger for my pastor to take a sword and to hew a wicked elder or deacon to pieces before the Lord. But that is part of the Old Testament picture which we must seek to understand and one to which we must return later.

NEW TESTAMENT INTERPRETATIONS OF THE OLD

There remains yet one more major way in which the New Testament has tended to get in the way of the Old, and that has to do with the way that Christian interpreters have tended to take later usage or interpretation of a passage as the correct and only possible one. In actual practice, this approach has meant that when a New Testament writer refers to an Old Testament passage this later interpretation becomes authoritative in a way that subtly implies that the study of the original passage is really no longer necessary. Such an attitude has tended to limit greatly the study of the Old Testament, for when someone studies an original Old Testament passage he may find that the Old Testament writer has given a different emphasis from that in the New. To illustrate, we could simply refer to the interpretation of Moses' killing of the Egyptian in Hebrews as compared with the original thrust of the story in Exodus. Inspired writers are often legitimately creative in their use of other inspired material, but to appeal to Hebrews, for example, as the source for the *original* as well as the *final* meaning of the Exodus passage is quite inappropriate. Yet Christian interpreters are strongly tempted to do just that type of thing.

Perhaps the classic example of a New Testament interpretation getting in the way of an Old Testament passage is Matthew's use of Isaiah 7:14 as a proof text for the Virgin Birth in Matthew 1:22,23. Conservative Christians have always appealed to Matthew 1 as one of the passages that establishes the Virgin Birth. And the meaning in Matthew is clear: Jesus was born of a virgin. But the interpretation of Isaiah 7:14 is quite a different matter. If we try to read Isaiah 7 as an Old Testament man of Isaiah's day might have understood it, we are hard pressed to see how such a man could see in Isaiah's words a *clear* prophecy of the birth of Jesus Christ. The context of Isaiah 7 would, in fact, suggest that the child Immanuel was to be a sign in Isaiah's own day to the then reigning monarch, King Ahaz. When Matthew cites that passage he is giving a second meaning of the prophecy, one which 'fulfils' the original meaning, or in other words, fills the original prophecy full of new meaning. Matthew's use of the term 'fulfil' is a matter to which I shall return later (see chapter 7), but the point we need to make here is that to find out what Matthew meant we must read Matthew; to find out what Isaiah meant we must read Isaiah.

That conservative Christians have often opposed this principle either consciously or unconsciously, is illustrated by the fact that when the Revised Standard Version of the Old Testament was first published, considerable opposition arose in connection with its treatment of Isaiah 7:14. The King James Version had used the term 'virgin' in Isaiah 7:14 as well as in Matthew 1:23; thus the language of the 'prophecy' and 'fulfilment' matched up quite nicely. But the RSV translators rightly retained 'virgin' in Matthew while choosing to use 'young woman' in Isaiah, a term which more accurately reflects the Hebrew original. In fact, there is a beautiful ambiguity about the Hebrew word *almah*, which allows both the original application in Isaiah's day and the secondary and more complete application to Mary the mother of Jesus. Yet the RSV translators were accused of tampering with the doctrine of the Virgin Birth by their translation of Isaiah. Irate Christians staged Bible burning parties in protest, evidence enough that feelings were strong.

This is not the place for an extensive study of the way in which the New Testament treats the Old Testament. But the examples we have cited illustrate the freedom which generally characterizes the style of the New Testament writers. I do not want to deny the biblical writers this freedom in interpreting and applying other biblical material, but I am concerned lest that freedom, originally a result of the Spirit's movement, should become an excuse for evading our responsibility to come to God's word, seeking a fresh knowledge of his will under the guidance of his Spirit.

When we allow each writer to speak for himself, we have taken a significant step towards relieving some of the problems that arise out of the differences between the Old Testament and the New. Scripture is much more like the full rich harmony of an orchestra than the single mono-tone blast from a trumpet. The many instruments, the different tones and harmonics, can symbolize the great variety of methods that God has used to work with man. As circumstances change, as people grow or degenerate, God moulds his message to the needs of the hour. For a people long enslaved in a pagan culture, the Sinai revelation was just what was needed—a little thunder and smoke to catch their attention. But as time went on, a fresh revelation became necessary to correct certain misconceptions about God and to shed fresh light on the path of his people. The beauty of that fresh revelation of God in Jesus Christ is something very precious to everyone who calls himself a Christian. But if we should be tempted to look *only* to this new revelation, we must then remind ourselves that Jesus himself made the startling claim that his Father was the God of the Old Testament, the God of Abraham, Isaac, and Jacob. And that was not all, for the Gospel of John suggests that Jesus himself was so bold as to claim that he was the great I AM, the God of Abraham (John 8:58). Thus there is no question that the two Testaments do belong together. But having said that, we must recognize that there are still two Testaments, each with its own particular message for us. So why should we allow the one to obscure the beauty and the truth of the other?

CHAPTER TWO

Behold it was very good—and then it all turned sour

And God saw everything that he had made, and
behold it was very good

(Genesis 1:31).

The Lord saw that the wickedness of man was
great in the earth . . .

(Genesis 6:5).

When I step back and try to picture the sweep of the entire Old Testament, and, in fact, of the whole Bible, I see something very similar to the scene suggested by the chapter title: a glorious idea that has somehow gone terribly wrong. I would hasten to add, however, that for all the wrongness and evil to which the Bible testifies, a generous portion of good still remains. And what is more, out of the wreckage of this beautiful creation God has conceived something even more beautiful and awe-inspiring: a plan of redemption, a theme that we shall look at more closely in chapter 7.

Because the Bible presents such an intricate tapestry, woven with the evil as well as the good, the horrible as well as the magnificent, a distorted view of the whole is quite possible. In fact, Christians have often shown a tendency to focus on one element or the other. Some have so greatly praised their Maker that they have neglected to take seriously the tragic consequences of sin. On the other hand, some have been so deeply scarred by sorrow and tragedy, that even the glories of a this-worldly sunset can scarcely quench the longing for a better world. The difference between these two emphases can be clearly seen in the contrasting hymn titles: 'This is my Father's world', yet 'I'm but a stranger here, heaven is my home'.

Any alert citizen of planet earth can testify that life is composed of the bitter and the sweet, the good and the bad, but it is a rarer gift to be able to enjoy this world while longing for a better one. To claim that this world is absolutely filthy is false. Nor can any sober person say that this little corner of the universe is a beauty spot which has no rival. For the Christian, a balanced view is vital: the thorns must not be allowed to ruin the roses, nor should the roses obscure the thorns. That is a principle which is significant not only for daily living, but equally for understanding the Old Testament.

In chapter 1, I noted briefly that one can use two rather different emphases in interpreting the Old Testament: the 'high road' approach and the 'low road'. 'High road' refers to an emphasis on the 'goodness' in the Old Testament, particularly in the lives of the men of God. The most straightforward example of this approach is found in Hebrews 11 where men of great variety and diverse experiences are all marked with the label 'faith.' By contrast, 'low road' refers to the approach which calls attention to the great depths to which the race of man had fallen, including those people that God claimed as his own.

Because the 'low road' approach has been so helpful in enabling me to come to grips with the Old Testament, I tend to emphasize that way of reading the biblical accounts. The 'high road' has marvellous potential for immediate inspiration, and perhaps that is why it has tended to predominate in Christian circles. But such an approach does not really prepare one for actually reading the Old Testament stories. In other words, one could become so accustomed to a 'high road' diet that reading the Old Testament itself could lead to indigestion! I think that both approaches are possible and useful, yet in actual practice it is difficult to follow them both with equal enthusiasm.

Perhaps one reason why the 'low road' approach has

been neglected stems from the recognition that the discovery of the shadow side of the Old Testament characters has not always produced positive results. In fact, the sins of the saints have often been turned against Scripture and its God and have been used as weapons to attack the authority of the Word of God. Nevertheless, the 'low road' approach is in some ways a two-edged sword which can cut either way. For example, one could turn to any nineteenth century devotional writer who is defending the Bible against its detractors. To the statement, 'If your God condones things like that, then I want no part of your religion,' he can answer, 'But it is precisely that point that vindicates the word of God, for here we have a realistic picture of fallen man accompanied by a picture of a God who stoops to help.' So what is taken as a great hindrance to faith by one man is seen as a pillar of faith by another. The psychological and sociological reasons behind those two opposite reactions to the same evidence are undoubtedly complex and cannot be explored here. But I do think it is important to recognize that there is much in the Old Testament that offends refined tastes. When we ignore those aspects, we lay the groundwork for the loss of faith. We must take them seriously and show how God can bring about his purposes even out of that kind of situation.

The 'high road' approach has often led to the aggravation of one more point of tension in the interpretation of the Old Testament, namely, that between those who see the religious experience of the Old Testament as evolving naturally, and those who see it as stemming from divine revelation. Much of the modern scholarly study of the Old Testament is based on the assumption that every aspect of man's experience is evolving, following principles of natural development. In such circles, then, it has become quite standard procedure to describe Old Testament people as developing from the primitive towards the sophisticated, from superstitious beliefs to a mature, intelligent faith. In accordance with such a scheme, those parts of the Old Testament judged to be primitive are said to be most ancient, whereas the more 'developed' parts of scripture are said to be of later origin. Thus the stories of

Genesis 2 and 3, for example, are said to be early and primitive because God is depicted very much like a man: he walks in the garden, forms man of the dust of the earth, he operates on Adam and builds Eve. By contrast, Genesis 1 is said to be the very latest (and greatest) theology in the Old Testament, written towards the end of the Old Testament period, because God is depicted as transcendent, quite removed from the mundane affairs of life; he creates by his word and does not get his 'hands' dirty with the dust of man's creation.

A PARTIAL REVELATION OF GOD

Such an approach to the Old Testament has often been so completely foreign to conservative Christians that we have failed to take it as a serious effort to explain some difficult aspects of the Old Testament. Conservative Christians have often tended simply to quote the New Testament view of the Old Testament and to use the 'high road' approach for purposes of affirming faith in God and in his word without seriously attempting to explain the Old Testament. The spectre of an evolutionary approach to the Old Testament has often made it impossible for conservative Christians even to listen to scholarly discussions about the Old Testament, to say nothing of actually participating in the dialogue.

At the risk of sounding terribly conservative to some of my scholarly friends and dangerously liberal to some of my conservative friends, I would like to propose, as a first step towards understanding the Old Testament, that we simply accept the scheme of 'history' which the Old Testament itself suggests. I don't think that is asking too much, regardless of whether one assumes a scholarly or a devotional approach to the Old Testament, or whether one happens to be liberal or conservative.

Now if we do let the Old Testament speak for itself, a rather surprising picture emerges; surprising, at least, for one who has been accustomed to taking an exclusively 'high road' approach to the Old Testament. Perhaps a brief summary can serve as an outline of the discussion which follows:

1. God creates a perfect world and calls it good (Genesis 1).
2. Man exercises his free will to turn against God (Genesis 2–3).
3. After the 'fall,' God's beautiful world is marred by repeated outbreaks of sin and tragedy:
   A. Cain murders his brother (Gen. 4:1–16),
   B. Cain's line develops into a hateful and hated race (Gen. 4:17–24),
   C. Noah's generation rebels, leading to the Flood (Genesis 6–8),
   D. Noah's son Ham mocks his father (Gen. 9:20–28),
   E. The Tower of Babel shows man still rebellious (Genesis 11),
   F. Abraham's own family worship other gods (Josh. 24:2).
4. With Abraham, God begins a fresh attempt to reveal himself to mankind, to a race of men which now knows very little of God's original plan (Genesis 12).

This prologue to the Old Testament is extremely important for understanding what follows, for it sets the stage for all the degenerate and 'primitive' acts which follow. Beginning with Abraham, God seeks to re-establish his way in human hearts, hearts which have fallen far from the natural purity and knowledge of the first human pair.

Now right at this point I would like to note a more serious problem that arises out of the 'high road' emphasis, namely, the assumption that virtually the full content of the 'gospel' was both known and essentially preserved from the time of creation through the line of the 'sons of God' (the patriarchal line). Whatever the reasons for that view, it causes real problems when one observes the behaviour and ethical standards held at various points throughout the Old Testament period. Christians have always claimed that what one believes about God has a direct impact on the way one lives. In other words, good theology leads to a noble life. If that principle holds true, as I think it must if Christian theology is to make any sense at all, then how could it be that the Old Testament saints had in their possession virtually the complete 'gospel' while their behaviour falls far short of such a theology? All the evidence of Genesis suggests that Abraham did not consider it wrong to take a second wife. His loss of faith was wrong and that he himself came to realize this is clear from the Genesis story. But the principle of polygamy is never discussed. In the Jacob story it is even more evident that polygamy is an accepted way of life. By reading between the lines in the light of later Christian standards we can certainly surmise the tragedies caused by polygamy, but Genesis does not moralize about it. To cite further examples, Exodus does not moralize about slavery, nor does the Old Testament grant an 'enlightened' status to women.

This tension between theology and ethics evaporates if we read the Old Testament in its original setting and do not insist on finding full-blown New Testament standards everywhere in the Old Testament. In fact, the New Testament itself contrasts the many and various ways of the Old Testament with the way of Jesus Christ (Heb. 1:1–2) and speaks of the shadow pointing to the reality (Heb. 10:1). Perhaps we could even borrow another famous New Testament phrase: 'seeing through a glass darkly' (1 Cor. 13:12). A type is never as clear as the reality, nor is the shadow as clear as the subject itself. Why then should we insist that the Old Testament be as clear as the New in its picture of God? For all practical purposes, the New Testament contradicts the claim of a complete Old Testament revelation while confirming that the Old Testament believer had quite adequate evidence on which to base faith (cf. John 5:46–47).

The point of all this is to emphasize that if one is going to understand the Old Testament, one must let the Old Testament speak for itself, something which conservative Christians have had considerable difficulty in doing.

Returning then to our survey of the Old Testament story, I would like to suggest, in keeping with the evidence from Genesis, that Abraham's actual knowledge about God was most likely quite limited. He was a great man of faith who acted on the evidence which he had. And though his knowledge of God was limited, and though he was occasionally unfaithful to that knowledge, he rightly stands as one of the great heroes of faith. The story in Genesis 22 of his willingness to offer up Isaac, the son of promise, stands out as one of the great testimonies to his relationship with his God. Yet right here within this great story of Abraham's faith lies a problem for us if we take the 'high road' approach. Biblical narratives detailing the later history of God's people clearly establish that human sacrifice was forbidden. If Abraham already knew that such 'killing' was wrong, then why should we commend his faith for his willingness to do what he believed to be wrong? Such an approach puts Abraham and us in an inconsistent position. What would hinder God from coming to me now and asking me to 'sacrifice' my child? And how would I know that it was the voice of God if he had clearly indicated to me by other means that such sacrifice was wrong? Would he expect me to disobey him in order to obey him? Not at all.

The explanation lies in the recognition that Abraham was most likely surrounded by a culture which assumed that the sacrifice of the heir was the highest possible gift that one could offer to the gods. It was only that cultural background which made that particular test possible. But interestingly enough, if we interpret the story rather freely, we find in it the very heart of the gospel story, for, in effect, God comes to Abraham and tells him: 'Abraham, I appreciate your willingness, but you really cannot offer your son. Only I can offer my son. I will provide the sacrifice—there it is behind you.' Is that not what God says at the cross? 'No merely human sacrifice can ever be adequate— I will provide the gift that brings peace.' Did Abraham see the full story? Through a glass darkly, yes, but probably not in detail. I think that is the message of Genesis 22.

A great number of perplexities that crop up in connection with the patriarchs simply vanish when we recognise that these men had entered a world that had been greatly distorted by sin, so much so that the truths which God had originally entrusted to the human family had disappeared or had become greatly distorted by contact with pagan culture. It does not take a great deal of imagination to see how an original promise of a Messiah who must die for our sins could have become distorted into the practice of human sacrifice. No proof can be cited for such a development, of course, but such a possibility would certainly be in keeping with the known human tendency to transform the gift of God into a matter of our own works and pride.

THE PEOPLE OF GOD: RISE AND FALL

If we follow the Old Testament story further, we note that the period of drastic loss of the knowledge of God highlighted in Genesis 3–11 is not the only one of decline and degeneracy. The descendants of Jacob migrated to Egypt where they became enslaved for hundreds of years. The biblical account makes it clear that when the time came for God to deliver 'his' people, their spiritual condition was low indeed. While the knowledge of God had not been completely lost the book of Exodus does suggest that most of the people had virtually lost sight of the God who had revealed himself to Abraham, Isaac, and Jacob. No wonder that Moses' position as leader of these people was often quite tenuous; they were always on the verge of deserting this 'new' God for the old ones of Egypt. And when this rough lot of ex-slaves finally arrived at Sinai, the laws which God gave through Moses provide clear evidence that these people, cowering in mixed fear and awe about the mountain, were so deeply involved with cruel customs that instant abolition of such customs was out of the question. The best that could be done in some instances was a slight 'humanizing' of some of the more barbaric aspects. And I use the term 'humanizing' intentionally, for I think the laws of the Pentateuch must be seen, in the first instance, as revealing the kind of people God was dealing with, and then only in the second instance, as revealing the character of the God who had chosen these people. The thunder and smoke, the heavy hand, and the strange customs seen at Sinai, are often cited by God's detractors as evidence against him. Because of the 'high road' approach, many Christians also find these aspects troublesome even though they choose for other reasons to remain within the community of faith.

Later Old Testament writers make it clear that when human beings forget God, they also forget their fellow creatures, sinking to cruelty and abuse. So when God seeks to awaken a knowledge of himself in the hearts of a people thus degraded and alienated from him, he does not seek simply to make them more 'religious,' but also to make them more human. Judged by the cultures around ancient Israel, the laws given to Israel show remarkable signs of 'humanization.' God took this people, in spite of the many barbaric and cruel customs which they had adopted, and began to draw them to him. He wished to show them a better way. But if human beings are to be treated as real human beings who possess the power of choice, then the 'better way' must come gradually. Otherwise, they will exercise their freedom of choice and turn away from that which they do not understand. I shall return to this point later, for it is a crucial one, but now I simply want to make clear the 'rise and fall' of God's people as the Old Testament itself describes it. Up to the time of the Exodus, it is mostly 'fall', and that is why the 'low road' approach can be so helpful.

Before taking up the question as to why God allowed man to fall so low, I should perhaps draw attention briefly to some other 'low' points in the progression of the Old Testament narrative. Have you read the book of Judges lately? Maybe you haven't been brave enough. In chapter 6 we will discuss in some detail one of the frightful stories at the end of the book of Judges, but the whole of that period is one of apostasy, rebellion, and degeneration with very few glimmers of light. If unstable characters such as Samson and Jephthah were the best that God could find for his judges, you can imagine the condition of the rest of the people. At the beginning of the settlement period, even that fine young man Joshua, one who generally occupies a position of honour on the 'high road', sometimes acts in a shocking manner, at least when judged by our standards of right and wrong. Take the story in Joshua 10 as an example. When five Canaanite kings had been captured, Joshua commanded his men of war: 'Put your feet on the necks of these kings.' With a few words about the Lord's continuing presence and assistance, he then killed the kings and hung the corpses on five trees until sundown (Josh. 10:22–27). What would a modern Christian church do with a military leader who treated his enemies in such a way? Reflection on such questions simply emphasizes how far these great men of ages past were from holding the kinds of standards that we would consider right. Yet these were God's men and God chose to use them. What does that tell us about God? Either that God is very cruel—or that he is very patient. I much prefer the latter alternative, for that is the kind of God I find revealed in Jesus Christ. With that deep Christian bias which I readily admit, I choose the alternative which best fits the larger picture.

Glimpses of two other periods in the history of Israel should be sufficient to give at least the flavour of the Old Testament story. The key names are Hezekiah and Josiah during the period of the monarchy, and Ezra and Nehemiah from the post-exilic period. During the approximately four hundred years of Israel's monarchy, her religious experience was wildly erratic. Some great and good names do stand out, including those of Hezekiah and Josiah, both of whom initiated great religious reforms. Hezekiah's reform and Passover preceded Josiah's by about eighty years and are described at some length in 2 Chronicles 29–31. Why does the Chronicler give this story so much space? Perhaps because in Hezekiah's day, the Passover was quite a novel idea, so novel, in fact, that the priests could not consecrate themselves in time. Levites had to be drafted to help administer the sacrifices (2 Chron. 29:34). The Passover itself had to be delayed for a month so that everything could be done as the law required. The people were so taken with this 'new' thing that everyone agreed to extend the feast for another seven days (2 Chron. 30:23).

Now one might think that such a glorious Passover would establish the pattern for generations to come, but how does the biblical record describe conditions when Josiah came to power a few decades later? The Chronicler's detailing of Josiah's own development is most illuminating and deserves a closer look.

As told in 2 Chronicles 34, Josiah's religious experience grew as follows: he was only a lad of eight when he began to reign (v. 1), but he apparently did not begin to 'seek the God of David' until he was sixteen (v. 3). What had he been doing for religion before this? Use your imagination. The Bible doesn't say. After *beginning* to seek the God of David at the age of sixteen, he finally decided to do something concrete to establish the faith; he began to break down the the idols and destroy the pagan altars, but that didn't actually take place until he was twenty (vv. 3–7). One would think that by now he must have been a devout worshipper of the true God and would have had most aspects of the faith firmly under control. Not quite, for it was only when he was twenty-four years of age that he decided to restore the temple, the official place of worship (v. 8). While the temple renewal was under-way, Hilkiah the priest found the book of the law (v. 14). The Bible itself does not clearly identify the book that was found, but many scholars think it was the book of Deuteronomy, or at least part of it. In any event, Hilkiah brought the book to the king's secretary who in turn rushed it to the king. Whatever the precise contents may have been, the king was greatly surprised and shocked (v. 19). Can you imagine both the priest and the king being ignorant of the book of the law—and that so soon after Hezekiah's great reform? And if the king and priest were ignorant, what was the condition of the average citizen?

I can well remember my reaction when the events of 2 Chronicles 34 finally made an impression on my mind. My 'high road' picture of faithful kings, priests, and prophets, who held high the 'banner of truth', needed to be remodelled to fit the picture that the Old Testament itself gives. What a struggle it was for God to reveal himself to those people, people who so easily and so quickly fell so far.

Our last snapshot picture from the Old Testament comes after Israel had been dragged into Babylonian captivity—the just reward for her sins as the biblical account so clearly states. Nebuchadnezzar's final capture and destruction of Jerusalem is usually dated at 586; the first feeble group of returning exiles apparently headed back for Judah in 536, but morale was a problem. After a half-hearted attempt to rebuild the city and the temple, local opposition discouraged the people and they simply let the temple remain in ruins. Finally, around 520, under the inspiration provided by the prophets Zechariah and Haggai, a drive was begun which resulted in the completion of the temple.

We have no biblical narrative which describes what took place during the next few decades. All we know from the biblical account is that when Ezra arrived in Jerusalem in 458/57, the state of religion was appalling. He and Nehemiah worked together to restore the city walls and the faith of the people. But a most sobering insight is provided by the last chapter of Nehemiah. Ezra had now passed from the scene and Nehemiah has had to return to the court of the Persian king, though the biblical account does not explain why. Upon his return to Jerusalem some twelve years later, which would probably be no earlier than 425, Nehemiah was appalled by the conditions he found. Some of the very reforms that he and Ezra had established earlier had been reversed entirely. Read the story yourself in Nehemiah 13 and you will discover further evidence of the 'low road' on which Israel so often travelled! In Nehemiah's absence, the people had given over part of the temple to one of Israel's avowed enemies, Tobiah the Ammonite; the priests and Levites had simply been left to fend for themselves; the Sabbath had been disregarded; and the Israelites were still marrying foreign wives, contrary to God's law. That last point was precisely one that Ezra and Nehemiah had 'reformed' earlier.

Nehemiah's response to this multiple threat was vigorous and passionate. In his own words: 'I contended with them and cursed them and beat some of them and pulled out their hair; and I made them take an oath in the name of God . . .' (Neh. 13:25). Tough lines, those. But perhaps not too surprising considering the circumstances.

Descriptions of the history of Israel often suggest that the Babylonian captivity cured Israel once and for all of the worship of pagan deities and turned her to the religion of law, an emphasis that is altogether too clear by New Testament times. But even that religion of law was not easy to come by. The evidence from the Old Testament suggests that virtually throughout her history, even after the exile, God's people were mostly travelling the 'low road'. One could hardly accuse Israel of worshipping God wrongly when she was not even worshipping him at all! But that must have been the case more often than we have been inclined to admit.

After tracing the above scenario, we must now ask the question as to why God would allow such frightful degeneration. Why would he create a world and then let it slide away from him? Why would he choose a people and then not keep them close to him? Those questions have often been asked and they are the right ones to ask. The problem of evil and sin is an ominous cloud over our world. When God's children either cannot recognize or cannot understand his activity among men, they turn away from him. I do not presume to know the full answer, but I would like to suggest a way of interpreting God's activity that has helped me to see the Old Testament and the New Testament as part of a consistent revelation of a good God.

A COSMIC STRUGGLE BETWEEN GOOD AND EVIL

The claim of both the Old Testament and of the New is that God is all-powerful, all-knowing, and the source of everything good. How could such a God be the architect of this world with its sin and tragedy? The Bible does not really attempt to answer that question in a philosophical manner, but there are some hints in Scripture that point in the direction of a possible explanation of the course that this world has taken. When these hints are drawn together, a picture of a great cosmic drama begins to emerge. John Milton's *Paradise Lost* is perhaps the best known popularization of this drama, but the elements are present in Scripture, and Milton himself draws heavily on scriptural imagery. As the writings of C.S. Lewis attest, the motif is still popular in our modern era.

The drama centres on the great struggle between good and evil, between God and the Enemy of the good. The Old Testament treatment of this drama will be discussed more specifically in the next chapter, but the hints appear very early in the biblical narrative. The serpent of Genesis

3, although more crafty than any of God's other creatures, is somehow also God's opponent, raising questions about God's manner of dealing with man. He claims that God arbitrarily has withheld something good from man. Traditional Christianity has attributed personal qualities to this serpent and has depicted him as the Great Opponent of God, usually under the name of Satan or simply the Devil.

The suggestion of a great cosmic struggle between this Adversary and God is further amplified in the book of Job. The Adversary accuses God of favouritism, implying that God virtually has bribed Job to serve him; remove the hedge and Job's allegiance would simply evaporate. In short, the book of Job sets a drama in which the Adversary attacks the very heart of God's ways with man. If God is to prove his case, he must throw his man Job to the lions, so to speak. Job suffers, argues, talks back to a silent God, but never abandons his faith in God's justice. Thus through Job's endurance, God's character stands vindicated.

Two additional Old Testament passages, Isaiah 14: 12–15, the famous 'Lucifer' passage, and Ezekiel 28:11–19, both suggest further elements in the traditional Christian interpretation of the cosmic struggle. In particular, the aspect of selfish pride is prominent in both of these passages. It requires only a small step to arrive at the two great points of tension in this cosmic drama: the selfishness and pride of the Adversary over against God's self-sacrificing love, a contrast that has been much developed in the Christian understanding of the mission of Jesus.

The New Testament intensifies the focus on this cosmic drama. When the 'seventy' returned from their successful mission, Luke records that Jesus exclaimed: 'I saw Satan fall like lightning from heaven' (Luke 10:18). In addition, both Matthew and Luke record the personal confrontation between Jesus and the Adversary (Matthew 4; Luke 4). Both accounts hint at a cosmic significance when the devil offers the world to Jesus if he will fall down and worship him.

Much additional New Testament evidence could be cited, but for purposes of defining the cosmic struggle, the final book of the New Testament is one of the more important New Testament points of reference. Revelation 12–14, and 20, in particular, throw the struggle into bold relief; the dragon and Michael are at war (Rev. 12:7). The dragon is defeated and cast to earth where he pursues those that are faithful to God's commands (Rev. 12:17). The dragon carries on his warfare through the beast of Revelation 13. The beast and his allies attack virtually every part of God's realm. As the struggle climaxes, its religious character becomes more evident, for another beast follows in the authority of the first, demanding that all should *worship* the image of the beast or be killed (Rev. 13:15). Thus the human family is inevitably drawn into the struggle. Those who refuse the demands of the beast are described as saints who keep the commandments of God and the faith of Jesus (Rev. 14:12).

Throughout the book of Revelation the theme of judgment is prominent—a judgment which is ultimately for God and his holy ones and against the dragon and his demons. Revelation 14:6 declares that the hour of judgment has come and in the chapter which describes the final demise of the devil and his angels, Revelation 20, judgment is committed to the saints (Rev. 20:4). The language of confrontation simply dominates the book.

Now it is perhaps noteworthy that where this cosmic struggle is given any kind of content, the enemy accuses God of being arbitrary: in Genesis 3, God is accused of *arbitrarily* withholding something good from man. In Job, God is accused of *arbitrarily* favouring Job. Yet interestingly enough, these same passages suggest that God actually grants remarkable freedom: in Genesis, the power of choice and the right to rebel; in Job, the right of the Adversary viciously to attack Job, Job's family, and Job's possessions. In short, the biblical writers seem to present the evidence for a freedom-loving God who has no fears of granting freedom also to his creatures and even to the Adversary himself. But in the context of the great cosmic struggle, when the Adversary accuses God of being arbitary, the only possible way of putting the accusation to rest is for God to do precisely what he did in Job's case: he must throw Job to the lions. Refusal to let Satan attack Job would simply have left the accusation all the more believable, and the reputation of God's government all the more in doubt.

But now let us apply the above suggestions to the interpretation of biblical history as a whole. If the course of history can be seen to be taking place within a great cosmic struggle in which God is accused of governing in an arbitrary manner, then we have a hint as to how we might understand his willingness to create a good world—but then watch it fall into serious decay. Who would be the mastermind of that decay? The Adversary.

The suggestion that the Adversary is in some sense the master of this world as well as the mastermind behind its pain and agony, appears in the book of Job. At least when the sons of God gathered together, the Adversary reported that he had come from the earth. This may also be the origin of the references in the gospels to 'the ruler of this world' (John 12:31). The devil's willingness to 'concede' rulership to Jesus (for a price!) as noted in the temptation accounts also implies a certain demonic lordship over creation. Placing this demonic control in a framework similar to that provided by the book of Job, we can imagine that a good world has been thrown to the lions. Thus, the entire creation must endure a Job–like experience at the hands of the Adversary.

If God's ultimate authority is to be established, then the full impact of demonic rule must be allowed to develop. The 'benefits' and 'blessings' of demonic rule must be allowed to develop for all to see, if God's lordship is to be finally regained. So just as God had to remain silent during Job's agony, just as he allowed Satan to destroy Job's innocent children, just as God allowed circumstances to deteriorate to the point where Job's wife could say: 'Curse God and die,' so it is with the world which God has created. Demonic forces must be granted the right to rule. Man must be granted the right to rebel without the threat of immediate and sudden punishment. And so we have the tragic sequence of Genesis 3–11, a sombre reminder of the devastation caused by rebellion, but at the same time, a testimony to a God who loves freedom so much that he even grants us the privilege of ruining our lives and the lives of others.

Yet God has not abdicated completely his responsibilities and control. Just as he set limits on Satan's attack on Job, so he has put some limits on the spread of evil. And just as God finally broke his silence with Job, so he also came in a special way to Abraham to renew the knowledge of God and to lead Abraham into a new relationship as an example of what a divine-human relationship could mean. But if God is the kind of God who loves freedom, then he cannot force us to grow towards him. Growth can come only as we choose to respond to the divine invitation. That is why the Old Testament stories provide such a mysterious blending of good and evil. In some of the narratives the distinction between good and evil is clear enough: human beings simply failed, revolting against what they knew to be right. But in other cases, divine wisdom apparently saw that man was not yet ready for the next step upward. Reforms cannot be hasty, otherwise all can be lost. For freedom's sake, God had been willing to let the demons have a fair crack at his creation; now God must defeat the demons, the false deities who had inundated the earth.

If we apply this suggested interpretative framework to Abraham's situation, we can see that if God had moved too quickly in his attempt to win the heart of Abraham, Abraham would have had plenty of other 'gods' to choose from. He was by no means bound to serve the God who had called him from Ur of the Chaldees. There must have been many things that God desperately wanted to tell Abraham, but he didn't dare. Abraham was not yet ready to move from milk to meat!

Thus when the larger picture of a cosmic struggle forms the background of the Old Testament, I find it much easier to understand the activities of God. It now seems strange to me that the Old Testament God has the reputation of having a short fuse. A God of incredible patience is a much more accurate description. Judged by New Testament standards, life in the Old Testament was often at a very low ebb. Yet God was there—working, inviting, winning.

We must not assume, however, that the upward path was a continuous one once God had come to Abraham.

The graph actually looks much more like a roller-coaster ride! Freedom means we may grow or fall, depending on whether we respond to the divine invitation or turn from it. When one of God's children chooses to turn away, the memory of the divine presence can very easily fade completely. Very little time is required to obliterate even important traditions from the human experience. I have known families who have become alienated from the Christian community and have turned away, taking their children with them into isolation. Given a few years of such isolation, the children have no memory of that which had at one time been so important to their parents. So it is with the rebellions and apostasies in the Old Testament. The example cited earlier of the loss of the knowledge of God between Hezekiah and Josiah is almost the rule rather than the exception, more typical than remarkable, though still very much a tragedy.

To summarize the argument of this chapter, we can say that God did create a good world. In this world he placed free creatures. They chose to rebel and align themselves with the Adversary. His attacks on God set the stage for demonic rule, a rule which a freedom-loving God chose to allow as necessary evidence in the cosmic struggle between good and evil. The Old Testament gives ample evidence of the impact of the demonic rule. At the same time, however, it testifies to God's patient interest in his own people, a people through whom he hoped to demonstrate to the world that there is a God in heaven who is the source of everything good. God had much that he wanted to show and tell his people. As soon as they were ready, he passed on the good news. The tragedy was that they were so seldom ready. Yet God was still willing to watch and wait. That is the glory of the Old Testament and the glory of our God.

CHAPTER 3

Whatever happened to Satan
in the Old Testament?

Now the serpent was more subtle than any
other wild creature that the Lord God had made
(*Genesis 3:1*).

If the suggestion developed in the last chapter is correct,
it would be quite appropriate to say that God created a
good world, but let it go wild. If he is a freedom-loving
God, his creatures must have the right to rebel, in spite of
all the tragic consequences that can come from such a
course. But then God seeks to win his creatures back. He
meets them where they are and seeks to draw them step
by step along a better path.

All that sounds fine—until I actually turn to the Old
Testament. There I find descriptions of God's activity that
make me very uncomfortable. At first sight, some of the
incidents seem to suggest that he is not a freedom-loving
God after all, but is quite arbitrary. Let's note some of the
more disturbing problems.

In the story of the Exodus from Egypt, the biblical
account says on more than one occasion that 'God
hardened Pharaoh's heart' (Ex. 7:3; 9:12). Now that
sounds like something much more appropriate to Satan
than to a good God. Why would God want to harden a
man's heart, setting him on a self-destructive course
which would also bring others to ruin? Taken at face
value, the words present a real problem for those of us
who claim that God is good.

A story that is perhaps even more curious is found in 2 Samuel 24. It deals with a census ordered by King David. Although the biblical story does not offer an explanation, David was apparently keen to find out just how large an army he could field, an act that would have been seen in that era as stemming from wrongful pride. Even his crusty general Job knew such a course to be wrong (2 Sam. 24:3), but David went ahead. According to the story in 2 Samuel, even though David belatedly confessed his sin, the Lord announced to David through the prophet Gad that punishment was on the way, though David would have the 'privilege' of choosing the mode of punishment. All that seems a bit strange to us, but the most difficult part of the whole story is the introduction which explains God's role in the incident: 'Again the anger of the Lord was kindled against Israel, and he incited David against them saying, "Go, number Israel and Judah" ' (2 Sam. 24:1). Then, as noted above, the Lord punished David for his act (2 Sam. 24:10ff). Now how could a good God actually incite a wrong act which that same God would then proceed to punish? From our point of view the story is inexplicable.

Moving to a slightly different type of incident, we could list numerous examples of God's stepping in and directly administering punishment. We might be more comfortable with a view which says that God *allows* the sinner to receive the punishment which his sin merits. Why does God have to wade in with his own scorpions and serpents? Does not sin bring its own punishment? One example should be sufficient to illustrate the point. Numbers 21 describes one of Israel's repeated rebellions. Rather than providing a picture of a God who reluctantly allows his people to flaunt his protecting care, to be pummelled about by the harsh realities of life, the biblical writer gives us a quick glimpse of the anger of the Lord: 'Then the Lord sent fiery serpents among the people and they bit the people so that many people of Israel died' (Num. 21:6). This type of description has led some to conclude that the Old Testament God is indeed arbitrary: 'If you don't do it my way, I'll send out my serpents to bite you.' Some Christians react against such a picture, while others actually use these very passages to shore up an authoritarian view of religious life: 'Don't ask any questions. Do it because I say so.'

Now in each of the examples noted above, if I simply take the words at face value without placing the incidents in a larger framework, the resultant view of the Old Testament God can be a harsh one indeed. That is why it is so important to develop the overall framework within which we can interpret the Old Testament. In the last chapter I suggested that the great degeneracy evident in the Old Testament is to be understood against the background of a great cosmic struggle between good and evil. That the universe may be more secure in the end, God provides the freedom necessary for evil to develop. The process is slow and dangerous when viewed from a human point of view and it seems as though God is taking great risks with his reputation. But the end result is the vindication of God against all the accusations of his Adversary.

Yet even if one accepts that type of framework within which one may interpret the Old Testament, one of the great surprises in the actual reading of Scripture is the very poor publicity which the Adversary receives in the Old Testament. In fact, in his place I think I would complain rather vigorously. There are hints of his activities in such places as Genesis 3 and of course in the book of Job, but if you really make a careful search of the Old Testament, specific references to the demonic, to Satan, or the Devil are very sparse indeed. As a matter of fact, a concordance will reveal only three passages in all of the Old Testament where a specific demonic being named Satan appears: Job 1–2, 1 Chron. 21:1, and Zech. 3:1–2. Traditional Christian theology assigns a fairly significant role to Satan, and he certainly is quite prominent in the New Testament. Why then does he have such a low profile in the Old Testament?

Before exploring the possible reasons for Satan's infrequent appearance in the Old Testament, we need to take a closer look at the Old Testament word for 'Satan.' The English word 'satan' is in fact a straight transliteration of the Hebrew word *satan*. And though the word normally suggests to us a supreme evil personality, Satan with a capital 'S', the earlier Old Testament usage applies the term to any 'adversary' or 'accuser'. For example, when Solomon turned away from God, 'The Lord raised up an *adversary* (*satan*) against Solomon, Hadad the Edomite' (1 Kings 11:14). The RSV has translated the Hebrew word *satan* as 'adversary' and it clearly refers to a human being. Likewise, when the Philistines went up to battle against Israel, a number of the leaders were reluctant to have David join them, even though he had been living in their midst: 'Lest in the battle he become an *adversary* (*satan*) to us' (1 Sam. 29:4). So David could turn into a 'satan'! But perhaps the most fascinating use of the word is in the story of Balaam. There the angel of the Lord opposed Balaam and 'took his stand in the way as his *adversary* (*satan*) '(Num. 22:22). Thus the biblical writers could apply the word *satan* to Hadad, an enemy of Solomon, to David, and to the angel of the Lord. But in each of these incidents the word simply means something like 'adversary' as most of our English translations indicate.

In the later use of the term, biblical writers begin to think of a supreme Adversary, *the* Satan with a capital 'S', representing the great opponent of God. But many Bible scholars hold that even in the three Old Testament passages where the Hebrew word *satan* clearly refers to an individual superhuman adversary, the English word 'satan' should still be written with a lower case 's'. The seeds of the New Testament understanding of Satan are clearly there, but Satan's supreme status as chief of all demons is not yet really clear.

Now when we cite evidence suggesting that the Old Testament understanding of Satan developed gradually, we need to remind ourselves that God has not given all truths to all men at all times. If Old Testament people have fallen far from God, then we must not expect everyone everywhere to have the same understanding. The Old Testament was written over a long period of time and this is reflected in the way that the various writers describe God's activities. A single event may be described by two later writers, both quite removed in time from the original event. The emphasis and interpretation of each writer will reflect his own special circumstances and, at times, two accounts may even appear to be contradictory. But if we make the necessary adjustments for time and place, we can discover the underlying harmony that is important for understanding God's activities. Perhaps the best examples of differing emphasis and interpretation is provided in the comparison between Samuel–Kings and Chronicles in the Old Testament, and in the comparison of the gospels in the New.

Now as far as Satan's role in the Old Testament is concerned, both Jewish and Christian writers have assumed the presence of Satan in many biblical incidents even though the original Old Testament accounts do not mention him. But both the original account without Satan and the later interpretation with Satan can be very useful. One writer has simply chosen to define the role of the demonic, while the other has elected to focus on the omnipotence of God.

If, however, the demonic is indeed a force to be reckoned with in life, the existence of the Devil cannot depend on whether or not a given writer mentions him. Either Satan has been at work in the history of this world or he has not. Without question, traditional Christian doctrine assigns a definite role to Satan. Hence the pertinence of the question: Whatever has happened to Satan in the Old Testament?

DANGERS OF EMPHASIZING THE DEMONIC

As a first step in answering that question, perhaps we could ask about the possible dangers that might arise in a primitive society from an emphasis on the demonic. By looking at various primitive cultures where the demonic plays a much more visible role, we can discover some interesting implications. Pagan religions are often dominated by fear. By definition, demons or evil deities cannot be trusted, so primitive people took all manner of superstitious precautions to protect themselves from the demonic. In ancient Israel, however, the use of magic and consultation with 'wizards that peep and mutter' was strictly forbidden (cf. Lev. 19:31; Is. 8:19). Israel's God could be trusted. Such trust, however, was not possible when the authority of demons held sway.

From a more strictly theological point of view, an active awareness of the demonic runs the risk of developing into polytheism or dualism. Ancient Israel emerged from a thoroughly polytheistic society in Egypt. Had God chosen to highlight the role of a satanic figure, the condition of the people could have made dualism, if not polytheism, a likely threat to the purity of the faith that God was seeking to establish. Thus the wording of the first command at Sinai may be more significant than a superficial reading might suggest: 'You shall have no other gods before me' (Ex. 20:3). Note that in this instance, God does not expressly deny the existence of other gods. He simply asks that Israel worship him exclusively. Other passages in Scripture greatly ridicule the worship of other gods and the worship of idols (cf. Deut. 29:16–17; Is. 44:9–20), but the evidence from the Old Testament is that the people in general had a difficult time focusing their attention on the one true God. Even when they were right with him, the threat of neighbouring deities was a real one. Thus, for practical reasons, God treated Israel very much as a wise father might treat a young son if the two of them were to set out on a jaunt through the woods. To warn a small lad of wildcats, bears, and snakes, could be quite unsettling. So the father simply says: 'Trust me. Whatever happens, I will take care of it.'

That is very much what I see happening at Sinai and in much of the Old Testament. The first great step that God asked Israel to take was: 'Worship the one God who brought you out of Egypt.' The knowledge about Satan would have to come later when their faith was more stable. And this late appearance of Satan seems to be precisely what we find in the Old Testament, for as we look at the three Old Testament passages where a specific *satan* is mentioned as God's opponent, in each case, the passage appears in a book that was either written or canonized late in the Old Testament period. But the question of early and late and the matter of canonization requires at least a brief explanation before we proceed.

CAN WE DATE OLD TESTAMENT MATERIAL?

Any attempt actually to date Old Testament material is fraught with difficulty, for the Old Testament books themselves give very little direct information about the time of writing. The only clearcut dating material comes from the prophetic books where specific prophetic oracles are often assigned to the reign of a specific king (e.g. Jer. 25:1; 26:1; 27:1). But a great many of the Old Testament books remain anonymous. In some cases earlier stories are retold, as when the book of Chronicles retells some of the stories from Samuel and Kings. But how do we know that Chronicles is retelling the stories of Kings and not the other way around? That is particularly a problem for the uninitiated reader who happens to be reading in Kings and finds references to the 'Book of the Chronicles of the Kings of Judah' (cf. 1 Kings 14:30). In this particular instance a more careful reading of the books of Kings and Chronicles clearly suggests that Kings comes before Chronicles and that the 'chronicles' mentioned in Kings are official court records, not our book of Chronicles in the Old Testament.

One of the more helpful ways at arriving at early and late for all of the biblical books, at least in a very general way, is to look at the canon of Scripture as held by the ancient Hebrews. Where the indications of the time of writing are slim, the place of a book within the canon can be enlightening. That term 'canon', however, also requires at least a brief explanation.

In its early usage, the word 'canon' simply means 'rule' or 'norm'. With reference to Scripture it means those books accepted by a particular community as authoritative, the books providing the norm or rule by which the community chooses to live. Other books may be held to be just as 'true' and in some cases just as 'inspired', but for reasons that are seldom known to us, the community did not accept them as canonical, that is, as permanently authoritative. Presumably there are sayings of Isaiah and Jeremiah, of Paul and of Jesus which did not find their way into our Scriptures, but are just as true and just as 'inspired' as the ones which did, or at least the early recipients of those words would have held them just as true and just as 'inspired'.

Protestant Christians generally accept the sixty-six books of the Old and New Testaments as their canon. Roman Catholics accept certain of the so-called Apocryphal books in addition. The Jewish believers accept only the thirty-nine Old Testament books (twenty-four by their reckoning), and even within those books the Jewish community sees different levels of authority, depending on the section in which a book appears. And that is the part that is of particular interest to us.

A New Testament reference actually identifies the three major sections of the Hebrew canon: 'the law of Moses, the prophets, and the psalms' (Luke 24:44). The process by which God worked among his people to designate particular books as 'Scripture' is one that will always remain mysterious. We must simply admit that the Spirit led the community of God's people to recognize certain books as containing the word of the Lord in a way that would be enduring for all time. The Old Testament canon was certainly complete by New Testament times as Luke 24:44 suggests. Furthermore, scholars would generally assign the following dates for each of the three sections: 400 BC for the Law (Genesis through Deuteronomy); 200 BC for the second section, the Prophets (Joshua, Judges, Samuel, Kings, Isaiah, Jeremiah, Ezekiel, Hosea-Malachi); and 100 BC for the third section, the Writings (designated in Luke by its largest book, Psalms: Ruth, Ezra to Song of Solomon, Lamentations, Daniel, Chronicles). These dates are really just educated guesses; the canonization of the various sections may have been complete earlier or later, but for our purposes it is significant to note that canonization took place in three steps and that it took place over a period of time.

It is also important to remember that canonization is not particularly concerned with authorship. A book may have been written long before it was canonized or a book may tell a story that happened many centuries before the book was finally accepted as canonical. At least the process of canonization gives us some guide as to when the community was willing to accept a particular book as authoritative for all time.

Now let us return to the three Old Testament passages which mention Satan and look at them in the light of the statement made earlier, namely, that the books in which these passages occur were either written or were canonized towards the end of the Old Testament period. A comment on each passage might prove helpful.

SATAN AND THE PROBLEM OF EVIL

1 Chronicles 21:1 Of the three passages, this one is in some ways the most important and interesting because it is part of the retelling of the story of David's census mentioned at the beginning of this chapter (2 Samuel 24). Not only is Chronicles in the third section of the Hebrew canon, but it is also the very last book in the Hebrew Bible. Hence it contains the very last interpretation of Old Testament material. And in fact the book of Chronicles is just that, a final interpretation of the period of the monarchy. In the course of retelling that story, the biblical writer makes a startling modification to the story of David's census. The earlier account said that the Lord (Yahweh) was responsible for the census, but in Chronicles: '*Satan* stood up against Israel, and incited David to number Israel' (1 Chron. 21:1). The inspired writer now sees that an Adversary was responsible for the evil deed, and not the Lord. A remarkable difference indeed.

Now if we are too concerned about harmonizing biblical accounts, we may miss the significance of this passage, so let us pause just a moment to consider the implications. There is a sense in which both passages can be seen to be true. If God is truly all-powerful, then he is ultimately responsible for everything that happens. Both the author of Chronicles and the author of Samuel would most assuredly agree with that. But whereas the earlier author was still operating with the view that the Lord is the *active cause* of everything, the later writer sees evil events happening with the *permission* of the Lord. Perhaps an illustration can clarify the point: instead of taking whip in hand to punish the children for munching green apples, the Lord allows them to receive the stomach ache which is the appropriate reward for eating forbidden fruit. And there is quite a difference in those two approaches.

I am much more comfortable with the way that 1 Chronicles tells the story, but I must also recognize the implications of the story as told in 2 Samuel, namely, that the Lord was willing to assume full responsibility for evil. Perhaps the reason was, as suggested above, his pastoral concern for his people. And if the Lord was willing thus to portray himself as responsible for evil, then suddenly we have a handle for understanding a whole group of problem passages in the Old Testament, including the hardening of Pharaoh's heart and the sending of the serpents. There is a sense in which the Lord is still responsible for all that happens; but now I have a biblical basis for saying that he *permits* instead of *causes* evil, even in those passages where he is actually described as causing it.

Now some may be uncomfortable with this approach and might suggest that I am putting my own interpretation on the words instead of taking the Bible 'just as it reads'. I will admit that I have put an interpretation on the biblical account. Upon reflection, we would probably all admit that every single word in Scripture, in fact, every word everywhere, must be interpreted. No word or sentence has meaning by itself. It is always read by a person with a particular background and infused with particular meaning. That is why 'father' can mean something quite different to me from what it does to someone else. When I hear the word 'father', I think of my Dad and have a very positive picture. But someone with a cruel father would see things quite differently.

So we must interpret Scripture. We have no choice. That is why the Christian admonition to approach Scripture always in the attitude of prayer is so very important. If I do not seek the Lord and ask him to guide me into the knowledge of himself, I will certainly misinterpret and misapply Scripture. When I come to interpret his Word I must use all the mental machinery that I can muster, but whether or not I use that machinery in the proper manner depends on my vision of God. It is not a question of faith or reason, but rather, whether or not I will choose to use my reason faithfully.

Now my reason tells me that there is a difference between 2 Samuel 24:1 and 1 Chronicles 21:1. The more I have reflected on that difference, the more significant it has become. As a matter of fact, you could perhaps 'blame' this entire book on those two verses. At least it would be safe to say that these two verses provided the catalyst for the method of interpretation which I am suggesting in the book. That was why I said earlier that, of the three passages which mention Satan in the Old Testament, 1 Chronicles 21:1 is the most significant one. That was a personal testimony.

Zechariah 3:1–2 This passage requires only a short comment. Although the book of Zechariah is in the second section of the Hebrew canon, the book itself provides the information which allows us to say that it was one of the very last of the prophetic books. In fact, it was written well after the close of the Babylonian exile. In this passage, Satan appears as the adversary of Joshua. The setting is evidently a judgment scene; the Lord rebukes the Adversary, restoring Joshua to right standing. Hence the passage provides a helpful illumination of the cosmic antagonism: the Lord is for us; the Adversary is against us. In the end, good triumphs as the Lord rebukes the Adversary and restores his people.

Job 1:6–12; 2:1–7 These verses in Job are certainly the best known of all the Old Testament passages which mention Satan. Scripture nowhere tells us who wrote the book of Job or when it was written. More traditional Christian writers have often tended to adopt the dominant Jewish tradition about the book, namely that Moses was its author. Actually, Jewish speculation about the book was wide-ranging. When the rabbis discussed the question of when Job lived, they propounded suggestions that ranged all the way from the time of the great patriarch Abraham to the post-exilic Persian period and the time of Esther. In fact, the rabbi who suggested that Job was a contemporary of Esther used a clever piece of logic which is likely to elude anyone who has not been immersed in rabbinic logic: Job lived in the time of Ahasuerus because the book of Job says that Job's daughters were the fairest in all the land. When was the time of fair women? The time of Esther. Therefore, Job lived at the time of Esther.[1] Perhaps it is not difficult to see why the tradition of Mosaic authorship seemed more convincing.

Regardless of who wrote the book, it appears in the third section of the Hebrew canon, suggesting that it was not accepted as authoritative until very late in the biblical period. The story itself bears every mark of being a most ancient one and perhaps it was the very mention of Satan that proved a hindrance to its general acceptance since Satan is not explicitly mentioned in the Law, and only once in a late prophetic book. Yet you will notice that Satan actually makes a very limited appearance even in the book of Job, a point which merits further comment.

One of the fascinating aspects of the book of Job lies in the fact that Job himself, his wife, and his friends, apparently know nothing of the satanic attack; at least there is no evidence for such knowledge in the book itself. Furthermore, when Job begins to realize the seriousness of his problem and when his friends attempt to needle him into repenting of his sins, sins which were non-existent from Job's point of view, Job argues with God, not with Satan. He clearly sees God as the author of his difficulties (cf. Job 16:7–17; 19:6–13). Even in one of the passages where Satan does appear, God says to Satan: 'You moved me against him, to destroy him without cause' (Job 2:3). So in the book of Job, the figure of Satan makes only a very cautious appearance. God is still responsible for what happens, and all the primary actors in the drama see God as all in all.

In looking a little more closely at the two passages where Satan does appear in Job, we must recognize how important the structure of the book is for its interpretation. The book of Job consists of a prose prologue (1–2) and a prose epilogue (42:7–17). In between is the poetic body of the book, consisting of a lively dialogue between Job

---

1 See the Babylonian Talmud: *Baba Bathra 15b*, English translation by the Soncino Press, London.

and 'friends' (3–31), a monologue by the young man Elihu (32–37), followed by the divine response out of the whirlwind (38–42:1–6). In the prologue there are five separate scenes, three depicting Job's situation on earth, interspersed with the two heavenly scenes where Satan and God discuss Job's integrity. Taking away scenes two and four, the ones where Satan appears, leaves the world scene as Job saw it. Only the addition of these two scenes gives the setting of the cosmic struggle between God and his Adversary, between good and evil. As is the case with every disaster scene in the earth, the causes and respons- ibility for the events are terribly difficult to untangle. We sometimes suffer because we deserve to, but often the troubles seem so undeserved. The book of Job attempts to provide some framework for handling the problem: a cosmic struggle in which the very character of God is under attack. We have already seen some evidence thus far in our discussion as to just how significant the cosmic struggle is for the method that I am suggesting one should use in approaching the Old Testament. The forces of evil must have their day in court if God is going to win in the end.

Before moving on to further implications of the disap- pearance of Satan from the Old Testament, I would like to comment just briefly on those passages in the Old Testa- ment which do not explicitly mention Satan but which have been interpreted within the Christian community as applying to Satan: Genesis 3; Isaiah 14:12–15; and Ezekiel 28:11–19.

In Genesis 3, an unbiased reader will strongly suspect the animosity which exists between the serpent and God, pointing in the direction of a full-fledged Adversary relationship. But the serpent figure is, in fact, an ambi- guous one in the Old Testament. The serpent attack recorded in Numbers 21 is successfully warded off by Moses' raising a brass serpent, the later symbol of the opponent of God! There is even evidence to suggest that the people began to worship this serpent; thus it had to be destroyed (2 Kings 18:4).

The first clear identification of the serpent as Satan in Judeo-Christian writings does not come until Revelation

12:9. There there is no doubt; the Dragon, the Serpent, the Devil, and Satan are all one and the same. Considering the strong role that the serpent plays in Christian interpretation, it is perhaps surprising that his identity is never really clarified in the Old Testament. An explanation might lie in the fact that in Egypt, the serpent is both a symbol of a good deity and of an evil one. The biblical writers thus could not really develop the serpent motif without raising the spectre of dualism or something worse.

Turning to Isaiah 14:12–15 and Ezekiel 28:11–19, we find two passages which share several similar characteristics. Both passages have been applied to the 'pre-history' of Satan and both appear in prophetic oracles or 'taunt-songs' against heathen kings. Isaiah 14 is directed against the king of Babylon; Ezekiel 28 is directed against the prince or king of Tyre. Modern scholarship has been very much intrigued with the parallels between these passages and similar passages in the literature of other Ancient Near Eastern cultures. Two general conclusions can be drawn from the research done on these passages. First, that the parallels in pagan cultures are striking indeed; second, that the prophets themselves are speaking of the historical enemies of Israel, not of the supernatural realm. The supernatural appears only by way of analogy. In other words, most modern scholars would say that these prophetic oracles would not have been understood by an Old Testament audience as describing Satan. That conclusion seems to be verified by the fact that the first clear application of the Lucifer passage, Isaiah 14:12–15, to Satan, was not made until the time of Tertullian, a church father who died in AD 240.

The history of the interpretation of Ezekiel 28:11–19 is less clear, for the passage has been applied not only to a supernatural being, but to the first man as well (cf. RSV), a problem of interpretation which stems from ambiguities in the original text. In any event, the application to Satan was apparently not made until several centuries into the Christian era.

The question naturally arises: is it legitimate to apply these passages to Satan when such was apparently not the intent of the original author? That is a difficult question to answer, for within the Christian tradition, an interpretation has often been drawn from a biblical passage which was clearly not the one intended by the original writer. A second meaning may have been implied, but that is quite a different matter from saying that such a meaning was the one intended by the original writer. Nevertheless, as long as we do not use a second application to obscure our study and understanding of the author's original intent, such second meanings can be useful. Certainly if we choose to stand within traditional Christianity we must be willing to admit that such secondary meanings have been very popular within the Christian community, and to a certain extent, we must be resigned to such an approach even if we aren't very happy with it. But the problem has been that such traditional interpretations have often obscured or even replaced the original meaning. I actually suspect that the vehemence with which traditional Christian positions are sometimes attacked is a direct result of Christian reluctance to admit the first meaning of the text. Thus, one of my concerns as I write this book, is to show that it is possible to stand within a conservative Christian tradition and still be able to read the Old Testament for the purpose of discovering its most likely original meaning.

But after admitting that the original intent of Isaiah 14:12–15 and Ezekiel 28: 11–19 was probably not to outline the pre-history of Satan, I still suspect that Satan is lurking somewhere in those passages. Connected with that suspicion is the probability that the prophets have apparently borrowed from cultures other than their own. We must make it clear, however, that prophets are free to 'borrow' whatever they choose and from wherever they might wish. It is the final product that is the result of the divine inspiration, not the bits and pieces. Yet even if that is the case, what right do we have to suspect that pagan religions had bits and pieces of a sort that could be used? That is where I think we ought to take the events of Genesis 3–11 more seriously. Whatever mankind may have originally known about the cosmic struggle would have certainly made its way into pagan cultures and would have come in a distorted fashion to that line of patriarchs which retained the slender thread of the

knowledge of the true God. Suddenly, here in prophetic
literature, bits and pieces of that cosmic struggle begin to
appear, but in a way which does not threaten God's first
concern, the development of faith in him as the one true
God. Certainly Isaiah 14:12–15 and Ezekiel 28:11–19 do
define the *issues* of the cosmic struggle, namely, that
selfishness and pride are the supreme distortion of the will
of God and lead inevitably towards full opposition to God
himself. The personality of the Adversary, however, is
certainly well hidden behind the mask of his quite human
protégés. Perhaps, then, the primary criticism of the
Christian usage of these passages stems from the impression that has often been given, that these passages must
have clearly outlined in the Old Testament audience the
knowledge of God's Adversary. Within the context of the
approach of this book, I would say that such a knowledge
was still too hot for the Old Testament to handle; it had to
come later.

One further passage should perhaps be added here
as touching on the demonic in the Old Testament, and
that is Leviticus 16, the chapter that describes the ritual
of the scapegoat (indicated in the RSV as the goat "for
Azazel"—Hebrew, *azazel*). Christian interpretation of this
passage has often seen both goats, the one that was
sacrificed and the one that was led into the wilderness, as
types of Christ. But another interpretation of this passage
with ancient as well as modern support suggests that the
goat led out for or to Azazel represents a demonic
element. This interpretation seems to find fairly early
confirmation from the intertestamental book known as 1
Enoch, for when the unknown author of 1 Enoch wished
to select a name for the leader of the fallen angelic spirits,
he chose the name Azazel. Now if the demonic element
was indeed part of the original ritual, then perhaps here is
an additional glimpse of the cosmic struggle between God
and his Adversary; one goat was for the Lord and one for
Azazel.

But after demonstrating just how little explicit information the Old Testament contains about Satan, we must
turn our attention to the way in which the Old Testament
writers handled the problem of evil in Satan's absence.
Although they would often simply attribute violent acts

directly to the Lord, they sometimes softened this picture by depicting other supernatural beings as the active agents in destroying and punishing. These beings belonged to a 'heavenly court' which was under the direction of God. The role of this 'heavenly court' is something that we must look at more closely.

If Satan's role is not clearly defined in the Old Testament, then we might also expect to find a description of the celestial economy which differs in some respects from the traditional Christian view which builds more directly on New Testament data. Revelation 12:9 provides the essentials of the New Testament view and the one which generally has been adopted in Christian interpretation: Michael and his angels versus the Dragon and his angels. The cosmic struggle is full-blown. In the Old Testament, however, everything must take place under the direction of the one God. Thus the 'dragon and his angels' must be seen to be under divine management, though we can still catch glimpses of their misbehaviour.

Perhaps an illustration from the human realm would be helpful in describing the difference between the Old Testament view and the New Testament one. In the New Testament, the forces of good seem almost to represent a government in exile; the rulership of this world has been usurped by the dragon, the ruler of this age. The tension is deep, leading to open war, as is evident in the battle-ground description of Revelation 12. In the Old Testament, however, the situation would perhaps be similar to the tension between two political parties, one in power, the other in opposition. Both still operate within the one government, but the opposition at times betrays signs of disloyalty to government policy. We shall return later to the Old Testament view, but first we need to look at another aspect of the Old Testament which is quite pertinent to our discussion, an aspect which is both intriguing and difficult, the names for God.

OLD TESTAMENT NAMES FOR GOD

As Christians, we are quite accustomed to the view that there is only one God. In my own case, for instance, I was so steeped in this belief, that it was surprising and difficult for me to recognize that for much of the Old Testament period, such a view was not so self-evident. I was aware that Israel's pagan neighbours worshipped other gods, but I had assumed that Israel clearly saw the absoluteness of the one God. To be sure, the Old Testament tells how Israel often turned aside to worship Baal; even with my 'high road' orientation, I recognized that. But what about Israel when she was right with God? How strong were her convictions then? That was the part that I found surprising. For even when Israel was right with God, she apparently tended to look at her God as the God of Israel, but perhaps not really the God of her neighbours. It is in this context that the discussion of the names of God in the Old Testament becomes pertinent.

One of the ten commandments declares that God's name is not to be taken in vain. The later Jewish community was so serious about that command that it decided the safest course would be simply never to utter the name of God at all. That habit of scrupulously avoiding the name of God established a tradition that has continued right down to this very day even in the Christian community. Thus users of the standard English translations (KJV, RSV, NEB, NIV) always read a substitute for the actual name of Israel's God. The story is a very complex one, but for our purposes we simply need to understand that, given Israel's situation in a world where there were many gods, the simple name 'God' was not specific enough for Israel's God. Thus, when God instructed Moses to lead Israel out of Egypt, he gave a personal name for Israel to use when addressing him, their own personal God. Most scholars now agree that this name was originally something like 'Yahweh'. Some modern translations (e.g. the Jerusalem Bible), actually use this name throughout the Old Testament, adding a most interesting flavour to familiar stories. Thus when we read the Old Testament, we discover that the Philistines had their Dagon, the Moabites had their Chemosh, the Syrians had their Rimmon, but Israel had Yahweh. And Israel also clearly understood that whatever the other nations claimed or believed, she herself was to have no other gods before this Yahweh.

Our modern English Bibles deliberately avoid using the name 'Yahweh', but by a very clever method, they do make it possible for the reader to know where an original Yahweh appears in the Hebrew: wherever you find LORD or GOD (written in small capital letters), that indicates the name Yahweh in the original Hebrew Bible. When you find 'Lord' applied to God (written with only the first letter capitalized), that is generally a translation of the word *Adonai*, a close equivalent to our English 'lord' in that it can refer to God or a human being, depending on the context; any authority figure could be an *adonai*. As for the word 'God' (written with only an initial capital), this represents the Hebrew *Elohim*. *Elohim* is like our English word 'god' in that it can refer to the one true God or to false gods. But *Elohim* is peculiar in that it is *plural* in form, so that precisely the same word could signify God, god, or gods, depending on the context. The above distinctions are important and can be quite helpful in illuminating some Old Testament passages; perhaps a diagram would be appropriate:

Usage in English Bibles		*Application to Hebrew Old Testament*
'LORD' or 'GOD'	=	'Yahweh' – the specific name of Israel's God, and can refer only to Israel's God.
'Lord'	=	'Adonai' – the general word for any authority figure; can be applied to God or to human beings.
'God'	=	'Elohim' – the general word for 'god'; plural in form, but can be plural or singular in meaning; only the context determines whether it should be translated as God, god, or gods.

The name 'Yahweh' as given to Moses is closely tied up with God's deliverance of his people from Egypt (Ex. 3:13–15; 6:2–8). This name had great potential for reminding

Israel of an intimate personal relationship, just as any personal name when used by close friends yields much more warmth than 'Mr.', 'Mrs.', or 'Ms.'. *Elohim* could be used to refer to God and was used a great deal, but it was the name 'Yahweh' that carried the personal message and was the one name that could never be misunderstood as belonging to another more ordinary god.

But for understanding the way that the Old Testament handles the problem of evil, the word *Elohim* is the important one. In many ways it is almost like our English word 'angel', but unlike the common use of our English word 'angel', *Elohim* is often used for the supreme God. In some passages in Scripture, the expression 'sons of God (*Elohim*)' shades into the supernatural sense of 'angels'. This is quite clearly the case in Job, not only in the prologue where the 'sons of the *Elohim*' met before the Lord, Satan among them (Job 1:6; 2:1), but also in the poetic portion where 'sons of God' and 'morning stars' are parallel, suggesting supernatural beings who sang at the creation of the earth (Job 28:7).

THE HEAVENLY COURT

It appears that these *Elohim* or sons of the *Elohim* are members of a heavenly court. In Job, Satan was one of these 'sons of God' and qualified as a member of the heavenly court even though he was clearly not a whole-hearted supporter of the heavenly government. That tension within the heavenly court also occurs in other places in the Old Testament, even when the figure of Satan does not appear. Of particular interest is the story of Micaiah and the false prophets, told both in 1 Kings 22 and in 2 Chronicles 18. Let us note some of the key features.

As the story is told in 1 Kings (the Chronicles version varies little), Jehoshaphat, king of Judah (the southern kingdom) has gone north to join Ahab, king of Israel (the northern kingdom) in an attempt to regain Ramoth Gilead for Israel from the Syrians. By reputation, Ahab ranks low as a worshipper of the true God, Yahweh, being constantly tempted by his wife's Baal worship. But the biblical writers generally give Jehoshaphat good marks for his efforts in the service of Yahweh. Why Jehoshaphat decided to link up with the ungodly Ahab is a curious matter, but he had done so. Yet having decided to help Ahab, the king's religious scruples began to work on his conscience. 'We need to inquire from Yahweh, first,' he said. 'No problem,' replied Ahab, and he summoned four hundred prophets, all of whom confidently declared, 'Yahweh will give Ramoth-Gilead into the hand of the king' (1 Kings 22:6).

These four hundred prophets apparently left Jehoshaphat even more uneasy, so he asked if perchance there might possibly be one more prophet. 'Well, yes, there is Micaiah,' admitted Ahab. 'But I hate him, for he never prophesies good concerning me, but evil.' Jehoshaphat got his wish, though, and Micaiah arrived, amidst a show of convincing visual aids by one of the other prophets—iron horns to push the Syrians (1 Kings 22:11).

With a touch of sarcasm, Micaiah told the king to go ahead (1 Kings 22:15), but Ahab caught the tone and commanded him to tell the truth. Micaiah did just that, confirming Ahab's suspicions as to the nature of Micaiah's prophecies, for he predicted the king's death. For our purposes, however, what is significant is the way that the heavenly court figures in Micaiah's reply.

Part of Micaiah's reply is couched in terms of a vision:

> 'I saw Yahweh sitting on his throne, and all the host of heaven standing beside him on his right hand and on his left, and Yahweh said, "Who will entice Ahab, that he may go up and fall at Ramoth-gilead?" And one said one thing, and another said another. Then a spirit came forward and stood before Yahweh, saying, "I will entice him." And Yahweh said to him, "By what means?" And he said, "I will go forth, and will be a lying spirit in the mouth of all his prophets." And he said, "You are to entice him, and you shall succeed; go forth and do so! Now therefore behold, Yahweh has put a lying spirit in the mouth of all these your prophets; Yahweh has spoken evil concerning you' (1 Kings 22:19–23).

The parallel with Job is striking, for though the Lord is still clearly responsible for what happens, the actual performance of the evil deed is carried out by a member of the heavenly court. But, of course, there is a notable difference between the experience of Ahab and that of Job, for Job is a blameless and upright man. Such is hardly the case with Ahab, even though the specific deed which precipitated his downfall is not indicated in connection with Micaiah's vision.

From our point of view, the charade of the heavenly court looking for some way to make Ahab fall seems a strange way for the God of the universe to carry on. But that is the beauty of a vision: God can use whatever imagery is necessary to get the point across in a particular circumstance. For ancient Israel, the scene of the heavenly court was very useful, for it maintained the view of the omnipotence of Yahweh, while allowing some of the deeds to be carried out by lesser members of his entourage. The evil spirit who misleads Ahab is not yet cast in the role of a 'satan' who is the 'accuser of the brethren,' but the picture is not all that far removed from such a view.

This idea of the heavenly court is used for another purpose in the Old Testament, namely to 'control' the gods of the other nations. It may be difficult for Christian theologians to visualize the gods of the other nations as something more than mere sticks and stones. Yet even in our modern era, conservative Christians can live quite comfortably with a belief in a demonic kingdom, while at the same time viewing all the gods of the pagans as non-existent. We probably wouldn't be quite so ready to say that the gods of the pagans were evil angels, but the Old Testament view is perhaps close to that point of view. Let us look at some of the key passages.

At the outset we need to recall a suggestion made earlier, namely, that God did not immediately set himself before Israel as the only true God of the universe. There are many passages in the Old Testament that declare that Yahweh is the only God worthy of the name. The creation account in Genesis 1 and numerous psalms declare that there is one God who made the world and all that is therein. But for the average Israelite the problem was faced at a much lower level: 'You shall have no other gods

(*Elohim*) before me.' Where do the other gods (*Elohim*) fit in? They are the gods (*Elohim*) of the other nations. Yahweh is the *Elohim* in Israel and for Israel; Dagon is the *Elohim* for Philistia, Chemosh is the *Elohim* for Moab, and so on. The biblical evidence for such a position is not extensive, but when brought together it provides a reasonably clear picture.

One of the most fascinating and pertinent passages is Deuteronomy 32:8–9, rendered in the RSV as follows:

> When the Most High gave to the nations their inheritance,
> when he separated the sons of men,
> he fixed the bounds of the people according to the number
>   of the sons of God.
> For the LORD's (Yahweh's) portion is his people.
> Jacob his allotted heritage.

So here is a poetic passage suggesting that Israel (Jacob) belongs to Yahweh, but the other peoples belong to the 'sons of God'. But you will notice a curious footnote in the RSV. The standard Hebrew text which was passed down through the official rabbinical line actually reads, 'he fixed the bounds of the peoples according to the sons of *Israel*,' a reading that makes very little sense and seems rather puzzling. The Septuagint (the Greek Old Testament), however, had rendered this passage as 'angels of God,' instead of 'sons of Israel', leading a number of scholars to surmise that in the original Hebrew, the phrase 'sons of God (*Elohim*)' had appeared. Apparently the devout and monotheistic scribes could not accept such an interpretation, so they modified the text to read 'sons of Israel.' But when the Dead Sea Scrolls came to light, one of the more sensational discoveries was a portion of a Hebrew manuscript with this passage included. In short, the conjecture of the scholars who had looked at the Greek Old Testament was proved correct; the manuscript read 'sons of God'. So the rendering given above by the RSV is most certainly correct and is one of the most helpful passages for establishing the Old Testament concept of the heavenly court.

Moving into narrative portions of the Old Testament, additional passages confirm the view that Israel sometimes saw Yahweh as one of the *Elohim* instead of the supreme and only *Elohim*. Judges 11:24 indicates that Jephthah, one of the judges, held such a view; at least such is indicated by his diplomatic correspondence with the Ammonites 'Will you not possess what Chemosh your *Elohim* gives you to possess? And all that *Yahweh* our *Elohim* has dispossessed before us, we will possess.'

This view is indicated also in the story of David. When he was fleeing from Saul, he had opportunity to kill the king, but settled for his spear and jar of water. When Saul realized what had happened, he and David carried on a moving conversation—across the valley from each other— but moving nevertheless. In his appeal to Saul, David makes the following pathetic observation:

> 'If it is *Yahweh* who has stirred you up against me, may he accept an offering; but if it is men, may they be cursed before *Yahweh*, for they have driven me out this day that I should have no share in the heritage of *Yahweh*, saying, 'Go, serve other *Elohim*.' (1 Sam. 26:19).

Driving David out of the land of Israel was tantamount to saying: 'Go serve other Elohim. You are no longer in Yahweh's land.'

Further hints of this view of the heavenly court appear in a most curious story in 2 Kings 3. The story describes Israel's attack against Moab. Moab was on the run as Israel pursued them right into Moab itself. In fact, circumstances had become so bleak for the Moabites that their king felt constrained to do something drastic: sacrifice the crown prince, his eldest son. When Israel saw this sacrifice taking place, they apparently recognized that here was *the* supreme sacrifice that a king could make to Chemosh. But note the strange way that the biblical writer has recorded the story for us:

> Then he took his eldest son who was to reign in his stead, and offered him for a burnt offering upon the wall. And there came great wrath upon Israel; and they withdrew from him and returned to their own land (2 Kings 3:27).

The biblical writer is apparently afraid to admit that Israel had granted any kind of power to Chemosh, yet he does tell us that the army hastened back to their own land. When we put this story alongside the other passages in the Old Testament which touch on the *Elohim*, the conclusion becomes clear that Israel's army was not at all sure that Yahweh was with them on foreign soil. Yahweh was *Elohim* in Israel, but was he also *Elohim* in Moab? They weren't taking any chances and headed for home.

Another story which has a bearing on the discussion is that of Naaman in 2 Kings 5. Naaman apparently felt that it was necessary to travel to Israel if he was to be healed by Israel's God. His testimony after his healing is remarkable, both with respect to the claims that he makes for Yahweh and for the parallel but somewhat contradictory recognition that back home in Syria Yahweh was not really in charge:

> 'Behold I know that there is no *Elohim* in all the earth but in Israel; so accept now a present from your servant.' But he said, 'As *Yahweh* lives, whom I serve, I will receive none.' And he urged him to take it, but he refused. Then Naaman said, 'If not, I pray you, let there be given to your servant two mules' burden of earth; for henceforth your servant will not offer burnt offering or sacrifice to any *Elohim* but *Yahweh*. In this matter may *Yahweh* pardon your servant: when my master goes into the house of Rimmon to worship there, leaning on my arm, and I bow myself in the house of Rimmon, when I bow myself in the house of Rimmon, *Yahweh* pardon your servant in this matter.' He said to him, 'Go in peace' (2 Kings 5:15–19).

Yahweh is the only true *Elohim*, but he is still the *Elohim* of Israel. Hence, some of Israel's land must be taken to Syria so that Naaman can worship Israel's *Elohim* properly, on Israel's land.

Still further evidence for the heavenly court comes from the book of Daniel. Daniel 10 describes how Daniel prayed for divine assistance. The angelic response was delayed because 'the prince of the kingdom of Persia withstood me twenty-one days; but Michael, one of the chief princes, came to help me, so I left him there with the prince of the kingdom of Persia' (Daniel 10:13). Daniel 10:20–21 also mentions the 'prince of Persia,' who will be followed by the 'prince of Greece.' Furthermore, Michael 'your prince contends by my side against these.' Now without the other evidence for the concept of the heavenly court in the Old Testament, one might be tempted to see these princes as mere human rulers. Yet the figure of Michael seems to suggest that we are, in fact, dealing with the supernatural. If that is the case, then the book of Daniel also reflects the concept of the heavenly court: Michael and Gabriel on Daniel's side against the Prince of Persia and the Prince of Greece. The tensions are deeper here, approaching the full break as seen in New Testament times, but the interesting thing from the standpoint of the heavenly court is the fact that each nation has its prince.

The crowning piece of evidence for the concept of the heavenly court is provided by Psalm 82. Without the concept of the heavenly court, the psalm is quite inexplicable, but when set against the background of the heavenly court it can be seen as a significant step towards the position which is so important to Christians, namely, that there is really only one *Elohim* worthy of the name, and that is Yahweh, the God of Israel.

This psalm is one of the best places to see the dual usage of *Elohim* as singular and as plural, for the psalm begins: 'God (*Elohim*) has taken his place in the divine council; in the midst of the gods (*Elohim*) he holds judgment' (Ps. 82:1). God then proceeds to condemn roundly these *Elohim* for failing to establish justice. They have judged unjustly, showing partiality to the wicked and failing to give justice to the weak, the fatherless, the afflicted and destitute. Then in a glorious climax which prepared the way for the exaltation of the one true God, the psalmist quotes his God:

> I say, You are gods, sons of the Most High, all of you; nevertheless you shall die like men, and fall like any prince' (Ps. 82:6–7).

So the reluctant members, the unjust members, the 'satans' in the heavenly court, are finally brought to justice for their failures. What then is the only conclusion that can be drawn? In the words of the psalmist:

> 'Arise, O God, judge the earth; for to thee belong all the nations!' (Ps. 82:8).

No longer will Naaman have to haul his mule loads of Israelite soil to worship the one true God. Cast down are Chemosh, Dagon, and Rimmon. Vanquished are the princes of Persia and Greece, for there is one God to whom all the nations belong, the God of Israel. That, of course, is a sentiment with which Christians would most heartily agree. Although the demonic is present in the world, there is one God who is over all, above all, and the creator of all that is.

Why did it take so long for Israel to see the truth? And why did God not make it clear all along? The answer lies in the character of our God. A freedom-loving God must grant his creatures the right to rebel. Furthermore, he must allow the principle of selfishness to manifest itself clearly if righteousness is ever to gain the upper hand. As God led Israel along the path of restoration, he sought to win the hearts and minds of his people. In a world permeated with polytheism, convincing Israel that there is one true God in heaven who is God over all was no easy task and the route may seem to us to have been circuitous. But as Israel grew towards the revelation of God in Jesus Christ, the principles of the great cosmic struggle began to emerge more clearly, until finally in the New Testament the issues and the key protagonists stood out in bold relief for all to see.

Nor should we overlook the significance of that New Testament climax as it is so vividly described in Revelation 12. The war in heaven and the thrusting out of the dragon is often seen only in its primeval significance, but the book of Revelation clearly sees the struggle climaxing at the cross. As the Devil is cast down to the earth a loud voice in heaven proclaims:

> 'Now the salvation and the power and the kingdom of our God and the authority of his Christ have come, for the accuser of our brethren has been thrown down, who accuses them day and night before our God. And they have conquered him by the blood of the Lamb and by the word of their testimony, for they loved not their lives even unto death' (Rev. 12:10–11).

The cosmic struggle may have been of long standing, but

regardless of when the war in heaven began, it was won at the cross. Though the skirmishes on earth must continue (cf. Rev. 12:12), the heavenly court has been purified and is now composed solely of Michael and his angels. The banished accuser is no longer one of the 'sons of God'. Thus, in a sense, Revelation 12 marks the transition between the Old Testament concept of the heavenly court and the New Testament portrayal of the battle between Christ and Satan, the great struggle for the hearts and lives of men—for the rulership of this world and the universe.

CHAPTER FOUR

Strange People need Strange Laws

'And what great nation is there, that has statutes and ordinances so righteous as all this law which I set before you this day?'

(Deuteronomy 4:8).

'Whoever curses his parents must be put to death'; 'If you take a second wife, be sure to treat the first one fairly'; 'Don't boil a baby goat in its mother's milk'; 'Don't let a Moabite join the church.'

Reading the Old Testament laws makes for fascinating reading—and disturbing, as well. Yet the Old Testament says that all these laws came from God. What kind of God would give laws like that? Before we attempt to answer that question, let's take a closer look at the laws noted above so that we can make sure that we understand the problems.

1) *The death penalty for cursing one's father or mother* (Ex. 21:17). Most of us would have no difficulty in agreeing that honouring one's father and mother is an essential concept. But if that relationship should break down, we would probably have second thoughts about the death penalty. Then, again, does this law constitute a clear basis for capital punishment for one who accepts the Old Testament as the word of God? Some Christians have not been at all reluctant to appeal to passages similar to this one in support of capital punishment. Maybe we need to think again.

2) *Fair and equal treatment for a first wife when a second one is taken* (Ex. 21:10). No one would quarrel with the

71

principle of fairness, but as expressed in this law, it is directly linked with bigamy. How can the great God of the universe give a law that condones bigamy? Yet the Old Testament clearly indicates that this law, too, came from God (cf. Ex. 21:1). Is he in favour of bigamy?

3) *Prohibition against boiling a baby goat in his mother's milk* (Ex. 34:26). Frankly, I have never been tempted to transgress this command, nor do I know many Christians who have. Of course, if one were to follow orthodox Jewish interpretation and use this command as the basis for not eating meat and milk together, life would become rather more complicated. Nevertheless, however one might attempt to interpret the law in a contemporary context, the fact remains that the biblical text itself provides absolutely no rationale for the law. Since most of us thrive on rational explanations, this unexplained law (along with many similar ones in the Old Testament) merits a place on our list of strange laws.

4) *Prohibition against allowing Ammonites and Moabites into the congregation, even unto the tenth generation* (Deut. 23:3). In this instance, the biblical passage does give a reason for the law, namely, that Moab and Ammon did not properly welcome Israel when she was coming into Canaan from Egypt. Perhaps a little punitive action would be justified under the circumstances, though to Christians who have accepted the New Testament's universal welcome to all nationalities (Gal. 3:29), this kind of exclusiveness seems rather strange. But that is not the primary reason why I have selected this law as an example of a strange Old Testament law. The curious thing about this law is that the history of its enforcement is so patchy. To be sure, Israel's whole experience was rather patchy, a point that I have emphasized before, but does that give license to break the law 'officially'? The law is included in the Pentateuch, but a major exception crops up during the period of the Judges, namely, in the story of Ruth the Moabitess. Now scholars are by no means agreed as to when the story was written; some think it was very early, others quite late. Since it appears in the third section of the Hebrew canon, we at least know that it did not become authoritative until relatively late. Ruth is included in the

royal Davidic lineage (Ruth 4:18–22) and her name also appears in Matthew's genealogy of Jesus (Matt. 1:5). Thus there is clear evidence that at least this one Moabitess was quite cheerfully accepted into the official community—ten generations or no ten generations. But to complicate the picture further, this very law became the focal point of the great post-exilic reforms under Ezra and Nehemiah. They insisted that the Jews put away all their foreign wives, Ammonites and Moabites included (Ezra 9–10; Neh. 13:23–27). Clearly, then, 'official' attitudes towards this law varied considerably. If we are inclined to think that an unchanging God gives only unchangeable laws, this law is indeed a strange one.

But after looking at these examples of strange laws, we must remind ourselves that Israel's great lawgiver, Moses, apparently found none of them strange or even burdensome. His buoyant appreciation of the entire body of Israelite law is found in Deuteronomy 4:1–8. In particular, note his claim that one of the great landmarks of Israel's experience lies in the fact that her God is near, ready and willing to be consulted. Furthermore, no other nation has received statutes and ordinances so righteous as the law which Moses has set before them (Deut. 4:7–8). So Moses thought of law as a great idea; good news, in fact. By contrast, Christians often have difficulty seeing law as good news, a matter which we must consider if we are to understand the function of law in the Christian community.

GOD'S LAW—ITS NEGATIVE CONSEQUENCES

As we begin to look at Christian attitudes towards law, we should take one more glance at the Old Testament and remind ourselves, that, even though Moses' attitude towards law was positive, the people under his direction were often less enthusiastic. They have our sympathies, for law does have a peculiar way of irritating human beings. Even the most docile and obedient souls must surely prefer to do what they want to do instead of what they have to do. Thus, when commanded or forbidden, we find it more difficult to perform or refrain, even though our natural inclination might have been to do precisely what the law indicated. I suspect that all of us have experienced this sudden withering of noble intentions when an injudicious command or an ill-timed reminder is laid on top of a good intention which had already issued from our own free will. Observant parents also soon learn that for encouraging rebellion in an otherwise good child, there is nothing quite like an admonition to do what the child was already doing or intending to do!

To illustrate another type of problem that we experience in connection with law, we could cite the example of speed limits. Now I don't mean those notorious and nonsensical limits which we sometimes meet and which seem to persist even though their very absurdity suggests they must have originated in some bureaucratic mix-up. I am referring to those necessary limits which all serious-minded drivers agree are necessary for the preservation of life. Drivers need the official reminder that a more leisurely pace is preferred in urban areas. But who among us hasn't chafed against a reasonable and necessary limit, simply because we are under the pressure of an urgent appointment? When it is our children who are walking to school on dangerous roads, we become quite vocal about the need for tougher speed laws. But when it is our urgent appointment that we are attempting to meet, the risk of killing or maiming a child somehow seems so very remote.

These then, are some of the human problems that we must face in connection with law, problems which God must cope with as he seeks to show us a better way of life. It is so easy to lose sight of law as good news and to focus instead on its potential to irritate. The New Testament itself is quite aware of this negative aspect of law. Paul, for example, in Romans 5–8, often seems ambivalent when he speaks of law, being aware of its negative potential as well as the positive. On the negative side, 'Law came in, to increase the trespass' (Rom. 5:20); and 'the very commandment which promised life proved to be death to me' (Rom. 7:10; cf. also 7:13). But on the positive side, Paul says, 'The commandment is holy and just and good' (Rom. 7:12), 'I agree that the law is good' (Rom. 7:16), and 'I delight in the law of God, in my inmost self' (Rom. 7:22).

One of the more uncomfortable functions of law is simply its role in pointing out sin (Rom. 7:7; cf. 4:15). Even though 1 Tim. 1:8–11 says that the law is for the disobedient rather than for the obedient, still, an awareness of law as the sinner's accuser hardly warms the heart of the saint! The answering grace of Christ strikes a much more responsive chord.

In addition to the 'natural' irritating and accusing aspects of law, the Jewish distortion of law also complicates our ability to view it positively. The gospels bristle with the tension between Jesus' attitude towards law and that of his Jewish antagonists. Instead of focusing on the mass of laws, Jesus sought to develop a healthier attitude towards law as a principle. Thus, when he was asked which was the greatest command, he simply said that there were two commands: 'Love God,' and 'Love your neighbour as yourself.' 'On these two commandments depend all the law and the prophets' (Matt. 22:40). By seeking thus to establish the priority of law as the basis for principled behaviour, Jesus saw himself, not as an opponent of law, but as its defender. To cite his well-known words from the Sermon on the Mount: 'Think not that I have come to abolish the law and the prophets; I have come not to abolish them but to fulfil them' (Matt. 5:17). In other words: 'I have come to fill the law full of the right kind of meaning.'

But perhaps the greatest significance of Jesus' statement about the two great commands lies in the fact that it provides a framework within which we can come to grips with all the individual laws of both Testaments. Note in particular: 'On these two commands depend all the law and the prophets.' All other commands are simply commentary on these two great commands and can in some way be subsumed under them. Paul refined this point a step further when, after mentioning several of the individual laws from the decalogue, he says, simply: 'Love is the fulfilling of the law' (Rom. 13:10). Thus law is not really ten commands, or even two, it is one principle, love. When we love, we are fulfilling all that is in the law. Love can never be rebellion against law or its negation; it is the embodiment of law in every act of life. An echo of this positive view of law can also be found in the book of James where the law is described as the 'law of liberty' (James 2:12).

We can conclude, then, that the New Testament gives ample evidence for viewing both laws and law as good news. But how can we understand and apply law in Christian experience so that we perceive it as something helpful rather than as something destructive and oppressive?

GOD'S LAW—A GRACIOUS GIFT

In attempting to answer that question, we need to look first to the body of laws in the Old Testament. Trying to make sense out of such a diverse mass is no easy task. There scarcely seems to be a way through that would not risk hopeless entanglement en route. The New Testament certainly provides plenty of evidence to demonstrate that such entanglement had become very much a reality, not just in the Jewish community, but in the Christian community as well. In the Gospels the argument about law repeatedly focuses on Jesus' attempts to establish a more 'human' approach to the Sabbath. In Acts, the famous Jerusalem conference provides at least a partial glimpse of the agony of the early Christian community as they wrestled with the problem of law: which of the commands of God were still valid for Christians who were not Jews (Acts 15)? The day of divine imperatives was clearly not past, but the 'which' and the 'how' were still very much discussed.

Given our difficulties in living comfortably with law, it is interesting to note the hints in both Testaments that God's ideal would be to eliminate the imperative in favour of the indicative. The clearest statement of this ideal is found in the New Covenant promise in Jeremiah 31:31–34. Here God looks forward to the time when the law will be written in the heart and it will no longer be necessary for each man to command or teach his neighbour, for everyone will know the Lord. Thus in the mature experience the imperative has been entirely transposed into the indicative. No external code threatens to arouse the natural combativeness of the human heart, for the heart is in harmony with the divine will.

But given conditions in a distorted human environment, the external law is a gracious condescension to the needs of immature creatures. Just as uncultured and uncouth children need more overt and explicit directions in the schoolroom, so human beings need more specific instructions to compensate for their lack of maturity. We can illustrate this process of greater specification by means of a simple diagram, based largely on the implications of Romans 13:8–14 and Matt. 22:36–40 as discussed above:

1 Command	Love	
2 Commands	Love to God	Love to Man
10 Commands	Commands 1–4 (Decalogue)	Commands 5–10
Many Commands	The additional commands in law and prophets which are applications of the 10, the 2, and the 1.	

Just as a maturing craftsman becomes less and less dependent on external instructions as the principles of his trade become more and more a part of him, so it is with the Christian and so it was with ancient Israel. With increasing maturity, the need for explicit law becomes less and less necessary. Conversely, as degeneration occurs, the need for explicit application of the great principles becomes more and more necessary. One of the more notable instances where Scripture actually defines this process involves the law on divorce. Jesus said that the law of divorce became necessary because of 'your hardness of heart,' but originally it was not so (Matt. 19:8). The greater the hardness of heart, the greater the need for more specific application of law. But this willingness of God to condescend to man's need and to give that more specific guidance is in no way a punishment for man's hard heart. Rather it is simply another one of God's gracious acts on behalf of his children.

GOD'S LAW—ITS PURPOSE DISTORTED

Yet in spite of God's good intentions, the history of the

Judeo-Christian tradition shows that this gracious condescension of God to the needs of people can very easily be misunderstood and misapplied. Even well-intentioned and conscientious people can relate to law in such a way that it leads to distortion of God's original purpose. The apostle Paul vigorously attacked one of the most dangerous distortions of law, namely, that obedience to law is a means of winning divine favour and gaining eternal life. Paul is quite certain that the law is good, but he never says that law is a means for obtaining favour with God. Law is a marvellous guide, but an impossible saviour.

Another distortion is more subtle, stemming from a misunderstanding of God's character. The logic of this distortion goes something like this: God does not change (cf. Mal. 3:6). These are God's laws. Therefore these laws do not change. In support of that conclusion one could even cite the words of Moses (Deut. 4:2) and John (Rev. 22:19): don't add and don't take away! If we adopt that view, then we face two alternatives: either that all laws are cumulative (the orthodox Jewish approach), or that laws apply for a specific pre-determined dispensation or period of time. The latter alternative is the one that has sometimes been adopted by Christians with the resulting interpretation that the corpus of law is applicable from Sinai to the cross. Then at the cross, either all the law, or all law except the decalogue, is abolished (cf. Col. 2:14 in popular interpretation).

The problem with that latter approach is that it conflicts with the evidence from both Testaments. The record of Jewish and Gentile behaviour as recorded in the book of Acts and especially in connection with the Jerusalem conference certainly indicates that the early Christian community did not see the cross destroying 'at a stroke' the provisions of the Old Testament law codes.

But the testimony of the Old Testament is even more telling, for here, within the same so-called dispensation, clear evidence can be cited that the laws given by God were not eternal. We have already cited the example of Ruth the Moabitess, but an even more striking example can be noted, namely the law concerning eunuchs. Deut. 23:1 seems to state unequivocally that only a complete and virile male could belong to the community. But Isaiah 56:3–5 gives quite a different thrust, for there the prophet reports the word of the Lord: 'To the eunuchs who keep my sabbaths, who choose the things that please me and hold fast my covenant, I will give in my house and within my walls a monument and a name better than sons and daughters.' This latter passage seems to be so much more in keeping with the Christian spirit, that we are inclined almost immediately to proclaim it as the more mature 'law'. The difference between Deuteronomy and Isaiah can scarcely be denied, but what possible reason could there be for the earlier law? The answer to that inquiry may stem from the great danger which Canaanite religion posed for Israel early in her experience. We now know from sources outside the Bible that Canaanite religion was violent and depraved, at least when judged by biblical standards. One of the customs that apparently prevailed was the practice of male castration, and that, in connection with the 'official' worship practices! There was real danger that Israel would attempt to imitate Canaanite practice. Hence the need for strong prohibitions, including categorical statements about male castration. With the passage of time and a diminishing of the direct threat from Canaanite religion, the necessarily harsh provisions of an earlier age could be superseded by more appropriate commands. Of course, the Isaiah passage does not explicitly say: 'This is a new provision to take the place of that old one.' Yet that seems to be just what happened. Jesus is perhaps using a similarly cautious approach in the famous story of the adulterous woman (John 7:53–8:11). He does not say that the law of stoning has been abolished, but rather: 'Neither do I condemn you; go and sin no more.'

The facts of the matter are that divine laws are no more enduring than that human situation which makes them necessary. The beauty of the divine condescension is precisely that God recognized the human condition and moulded his revelation accordingly. Different people in different cultures need to have the great enduring principles of divine government applied in different ways. But therein lies a particular problem that we must realize, for the greater the specificity in the commands the greater will be the likelihood of apparent conflict between such commands and the need for exceptions. In a sinful world, conflict can develop even at the level of the two great commands, love to God and love to man, for when a human command from colleague, parent, or magistrate runs counter to our responsibility to God, the two commands are superficially in tension. But only superficially, for the higher law of God (self-sacrificing love) is enduring and that must always be the final court of appeal. It is never 'necessary' to break the law; God's law is the law of life and it is eternal. To be true to that law is to be true to God himself and that is where our loyalties must always lie.

We must admit, however, that not all cases of apparent conflict can be easily resolved. The great issues of war and peace, life and death, and the complications raised by tyranny and oppression make the modern study of ethics very pertinent indeed. Nor will it do to solve the problems with a mere appeal to a specific statement of Scripture. Each passage of Scripture, each instance of biblical law, must be studied within its larger context to determine just how and why the larger principles of God's eternal law are to be applied in a distorted human context. Each bit and piece of God's revelation to man will tell us something about God and something about the people with whom he is dealing. Furthermore, the great variety of conditions and circumstances in which God meets man means that we have a great wealth of material for understanding both God and man. If we approach our problems today with an awareness of what has gone before, asking for the guidance of the Spirit, we will discover what God would have us be and how he would have us live.

STRANGE LAWS FOR STRANGE PEOPLE?

Perhaps a further word would be appropriate in connection with the rather more rigorous nature of Old Testament law. In particular, the death penalty was quite common. Conservative Christians have sometimes been reluctant to admit the great contrast between Old and New, perhaps because the image of an unchanging God is more congenial, at first glance, than the image of a God who condescends to enter the human arena. But if the New Testament can testify to a God who became flesh, cannot the Old Testament bear witness to a God who stoops even further in order to reach man? The Old Testament man was often violent; God had to meet him there and help him from there. The Old Testament reveals 'approved' customs that are nothing short of barbaric, but we can also detect the hand of God as he works through these customs to lead his people to higher ground. The human race had chosen the steep downward path away from God; the journey back must be via the same tortuous route. Going down is always so quick and easy; retracing one's steps upwards is so painful and so slow. But the God of the Old Testament would not negate the law of life. Growth comes by choosing the right. Step by step, God led his people at a pace which they could manage. The strange laws for these strange people are a marvellous testimony to a kind and patient God and provide a fitting background for the God who would one day reveal himself in Jesus Christ. Just as the New Testament would find Jesus and Mount Zion much more attractive than the terrors of Sinai (cf. Heb. 12:18–24), so we also will probably be more comfortable with Jesus of Nazareth than with the thunder and smoke of that desert mountain. But a closer look reveals a great God who knew that his first task was to impress that riotous mob of ex-slaves. And they were impressed, so much so, that they ran and hid and said that enough was enough. But perhaps their reaction was similar to that mixed fear and pride that a little boy has of his strapping big brother. Junior is afraid, but who wouldn't be delighted to have that kind of brother to beat off the neighbourhood bullies? So it was with Israel. They were afraid, but God had made his point and they were his.

Let us take a quick backward glance, then, at the four sample laws mentioned at the beginning of this chapter and summarize some of the implications that have surfaced in the course of our discussion.

1) *Death penalty for cursing one's father or mother* (Ex. 21:17). The value of honouring one's parents is clear enough, but the background of the Israelites included the death penalty. Was God in favour of the death penalty? Is he still? Any straightforward answer could easily be misleading. We must say, of course, that God is in favour of life; death is the result of sin. Maybe all that we can say with certainty is that God apparently was willing to make use of the death penalty when dealing with ancient Israel. Israel would not have accepted a God who did not enforce such 'standard' norms of justice. I suspect that the use of the death penalty was an accommodation to the condition of mankind at that time. Whether or not it should still be used today is a question which is still open for us to decide. Our prayer must be that we will make that decision under the guidance of the Spirit.

2) *Fair and equal treatment for a first wife when a second one is taken* (Ex. 21:10). Through the early patriarchal accounts the custom of multiple wives is evidently accepted without any qualms. It is not surprising, then, that God would include instructions as to how best to cope with a multiple-wife situation. Once we recognize the principle of accommodation to man's need, we need not conclude that God is actually in favour of bigamy. Perhaps it might be instructive, however, to explore the possibility of applying this very command today within those cultures where bigamy and polygamy are practised. Does this command suggest that where a multiple wife situation already exists, the status quo is in order? That is not an easy question to answer, but perhaps some agony of soul would be more appropriate than to conclude too hastily that the ultimate in Christian standards should be enforced in every place at all times. The problem will always be, however: how do we make the transition to the better way?

3) *Prohibition against boiling a baby goat in his mother's milk* (Ex. 34:26). Fairly recent discoveries have suggested that this law is directed against Canaanite fertility practices. It would then be in the same category as the law against a castrated male noted above (Deut. 23:1). When the threat posed by Canaanite religion had passed, the law would

also be irrelevant. Certain activities are wrong only because of the way that they might be understood in a given culture. There are basic principles in the law which certainly transcend human culture, but those basic principles also suggest that when we are within a particular culture we must avoid those things which would be offensive or which could possibly lead to a dangerous misunderstanding.

4) *Prohibition against admitting Moabites and Ammonites into the congregation* (Deut. 23:3). I have already noted how attitudes towards this law blew hot and cold. The potential threat of foreign influence against the true faith varied greatly from age to age. The most evident enforcement of this command took place in the post-exilic period during the reforms of Ezra and Nehemiah. Although the enforcement of the command at that time seems exceptionally harsh to us, we now know from sources outside the Bible that pagan influences threatened to compromise fatally the Jewish faith. Ezra and Nehemiah responded with vigour and enthusiasm, making use of this law as part of their reform.

Another point that we would do well to remember in connection with this law is that the Christian view of all being one in Christ has so conditioned us that we find it difficult to adjust to the more tribal and exclusive attitude in the Old Testament. Yet in a culture where tribal loyalties reign supreme, it is not surprising to find a persistent attitude of harshness towards one's enemies. The Old Testament denounces not only Moab and Ammon, but Israel's other enemies as well. Given these conditions, what is really so surprising is the appearance in the Old Testament of the story of Ruth the Moabitess, the ancestress of David and of Jesus. Even in the Old Testament, the higher law of love sometimes superseded those harsher commands which were a necessary adaptation to the needs of a people who had fallen far from God's ideal.

But after speaking so much of adaptation, of God's condescension to the needs of fallen human beings, I must strike a blow on behalf of permanence and continuity, qualities which seem to apply much more to the decalogue than to the subsidiary commands in the Old Testament. Defined carefully, the commands of the decalogue have a high degree of permanence. This higher priority for the decalogue has found confirmation in the Christian tradition and seems also to be confirmed in the Old Testament, for the tables of stone were placed within the ark of the covenant, while the additional Mosaic legislation was placed in the side of the ark. We must recognize, however, that simply because the decalogue has a higher degree of permanence for fallen man, the ethical questions which we face today are not thereby automatically solved. In fact, one of the primary implications of the approach to law suggested in this chapter is the absolutely crucial role it assigns to the human interpreter of law. The point is sufficiently important to merit another whole book, but I shall content myself here with a few comments on some of the more significant aspects.

GOD'S LAW AND HUMAN RESPONSIBILITY

Conservative Christians have sometimes been reluctant to grant human reason a prominent role in the decision-making process because to do so would imply that we are walking 'by sight' rather than 'by faith.' Such an approach, however, tends to place faith in opposition to reason, a most unfortunate conclusion, for the two should be walking hand in hand. Perhaps we can take some steps towards solving the difficulty by looking first at the decision-making process, and second, by seeing that process as a focal point in the cosmic struggle between good and evil.

Looking at the decision-making process, I find it helpful to note three basic elements in every decision: 1) The driving motive force behind the decision, usually love or selfishness or a mixture of the two; 2) The data base for the decision, including an awareness of relevant Scriptural contexts and a knowledge of the key factors in the modern context that have rendered a decision necessary. Additional information from many sources can be extremely important for substantiating and clarifying the data base.

Thus the full spectrum of the modern sciences as well as the more classical disciplines can greatly enhance our understanding both of the biblical record and of the contemporary scene; 3) The actual decision-making process, the reaction of the motive-force with the data. The process moves from recognition of the problem, through the data-gathering and evaluation, and finally to the conclusion and execution of the decision.

Now the first element, the motive force, is in many ways the determining factor for the decision, for it determines the degree of honesty and intensity with which one gathers, interprets and applies the data. If the motive is pure, we are much more likely to make a right decision. Yet, crucial as our motives are, the stark truth is that we are powerless to change or purify them. That is something that only the Spirit can do as we seek a clearer vision of God. Recognition of that sobering fact should lead me as a Christian to set my mind on the Spirit, rather than on the flesh (cf. Rom. 8:5). That is the only way that my decisions can be truly Christian.

But having set my mind on the Spirit, what does that do for the data gathering? Since I have now sought God's guidance in my decision-making I should be *more* thorough in collecting and evaluating the data. Far from negating my human responsibilities, being Spirit-led enhances and intensifies them. God gave me this mental machinery and he expects me to use it. I come to him so that he can purify my heart, my motives; that is something quite beyond me. But I do have capabilities for collecting and gathering data, for deciding, and then acting upon my decision. If the Lord is guiding my motive force, the whole process will be guided by him. And the beauty of this whole process is that God remains God and man remains man. I do not negate the purpose for which God created me, nor do I usurp the role that divine power must play in my experience.

Several distortions of this process are possible. First, I may fail to seek the Spirit, in which case, selfishness will dominate my motives and my decisions. Second, I may be operating on a legalistic basis in which no living decision-making process is necessary nor is the guidance of the

Spirit really needed; I just obey the law! But since no specific set of laws can really be adequate or foolproof in this twisted world, such a method leads either to a horrendous and hopeless multiplication of law (the rabbinic method), or to a cruel disregard for human need, or both. The classical biblical illustration of this distortion is the Jewish approach to the Sabbath. Jesus sought to show that the Sabbath was made for man and that it was lawful to do good on the Sabbath. In short, Jesus taught that human needs must be cared for through the Sabbath, not neglected because of the Sabbath.

The third distortion is one that is quite common among those who 'let the Lord lead'. I firmly believe that I must let the Lord lead me, and I have attempted to describe how I see him leading in the decision-making process. But it would be dereliction of my human responsibility to expect him to lead me as though I were a blind man, totally dependent on him not only to provide the motive force, but also to collect my data and to make my decision. I am totally dependent on him to cleanse my motives, but it is my responsibility to collect and evaluate the data under the guidance of the Spirit. I am sympathetic with those who believe that it is important that the Lord make their every decision and I do not wish to be overly critical. But I do think that when we take that approach, we are virtually stepping to the sidelines in the great cosmic struggle. That is why I see the decision-making process as being so crucial in the great struggle between good and evil. Let me explain further.

If the cosmic struggle is all about freedom, then I must exercise my freedom to choose for God. If I surrender my proper role in the decision-making process, even if I surrender it to God, then I am forsaking the arena at that point. Even the apparent vote for God that I am casting at that point is, in reality, a vote in favour of the Adversary. He has said all along that God does not really want me to think; that God would rather make all the decisions for me. But I refuse to support the Adversary! The God that I serve asks me to surrender my will to him, but never to relinguish my humanity. When I surrender my will, my humanity is vivified and renewed. My life becomes a living sacrifice in which my every act tells for or against God in the cosmic struggle. That is the great challenge in Christian living.

A glance at Job's experience can be helpful in this connection. He had to live and act for God even though he had no *visible* sign of God's presence. So it is for us. My choice for God when all is going well and when I feel him near is not nearly so significant as my choice for him when I feel God-forsaken. The world so often appears God-forsaken and deserted. God is so often silent when we cry out to him in desperation. But if in that loneliness, if in that awful silence, I can still choose to set my mind on the Spirit instead of on the flesh, then I can play a part in the vindication of God and his government. The knowledge that I can play even a small part for the great God who made me and one day wants me to be with him adds an element of excitement to this life that I wouldn't want to be without.

Of course, God has not always remained silent. Scripture is part of the evidence that he has been active on our behalf. And this very evidence in Scripture can shore up my confidence when God seems silent. In fact, I suspect that it was Jesus' awareness of Scripture that made it possible for him to move from his feelings of God-forsakenness to the point where he could say, 'Father, into thy hands I commend my spirit' (Luke 23:46).

That final serenity, that deep awareness of God's immediate presence is something that we all crave. God will grant it to us some day. But in the meantime, the war rages on, and we must have an understanding of God which will enable us to live for him with vigour and enthusiasm—even when he is silent. Every day brings myriads of decisions. God has given us the privilege of making our own decisions. He expects us to make our own decisions, but with our minds set on him. Whether he seems near or far, life goes on. We must simply choose to set our minds on the Spirit, and then use all of the talents that the Lord has given us, and use them to his glory.

In this chapter, I have attempted to discuss law in a way which will enable us to understand both the consistency of law in principle and the variety of law in application. That fascinating combination of consistency and variety is what keeps the whole body of law in Scripture alive for us today. Not that all the laws apply with equal validity. By no means! But law remains alive in the sense that we can see how God has dealt with man in the past and thus can learn how he deals with men today. And, as with all our study of Scripture, the mind must be set on the Spirit if we are to understand aright. But having done that, the very nature of the biblical law should alert me to the great danger of simply following specific laws. My mind and heart must always be alert, so that in every situation, my life and my decisions will lead to the fulfilment of that greatest of principles, the principle of love.

Speaking of that principle of love brings us to the capstone of our discussion of law: the relationship between Christian experience and the law. The question can be simply put. How can love take the sting out of the imperative? I may understand a great deal about God's activity in the past. I may even find that understanding to be a great help in the daily decisions that I must make. But sooner or later, I must come face to face with uncomfortable duty, with unwanted but necessary responsibility, with the divine imperative. Does God have a way of helping me to see my 'duty' in a way that does not arouse my natural hostility to the imperative? He does. Let us see how.

I have mentioned several times that God's willingness to reveal his law is part of his gracious activity on our behalf. But since laws come in the imperative mode they can so easily get our backs up. We simply don't like to be told to do something, even if it is for our own good. But as I have reflected on the way that God has dealt with man, I have discovered that he is quite aware of the nasty barbs that accompany law. If we will look at the larger picture of God's gracious activity we can see just how sensitive he has been to our need.

GRACE BEFORE LAW

This beautiful aspect of God's way with man can be

summarized in the phrase: 'grace before law'. Now that may sound strange to those of us who are accustomed to thinking of law as something which condemns, something which must be followed by the good news of saving grace. In that way of thinking, law is, of course, bad news. Furthermore if that is the way I insist on looking at law and grace, I will never make peace with law; it will always rub me up the wrong way. What then does 'grace before law' mean? Just this. When God comes to man, his first approach is not law, but grace. Before we ever do anything for him or even in response to him, grace is there as his free gift. The classic New Testament passage in this respect is Romans 5: 'While we were still weak' (vs. 6), 'while we were yet sinners' (vs. 8), 'while we were enemies' (vs. 10), 'we were reconciled to God by the death of his Son' (vs. 10). We did nothing to merit such a gift. While we were yet shaking our fist in God's face he did something that could touch our lives and make us whole. Once our lives have thus been touched by his goodness, we are able to recognize that this great God also wants to show us how to live and that his law is part of his plan for our life. But now the sting has been taken out of law because we have first been touched by grace. As the Gospel of John records: 'If you love me, you will keep my commandments' (John 14:15). If we let ourselves be touched by his love, we cannot help but love him and then the natural result is to follow in the path that he has given us for our happiness.

Now since this is a book about the Old Testament, I should hasten to add that the familiar picture of grace before law in the New Testament is paralleled in the Old, and right at the focal point of the Old Testament record, Israel's deliverance from Egypt. The amazing story of God's deliverance of his people shows that they had not one shred of merit to offer him. Even their faith was very much smaller than that of a mustard seed. But God delivered them from Egypt. He rolled back the waters of the sea. Then and only then, did he bring them to Sinai and the law. But it was the memory of God's mighty deliverance that placed that smoking mountain in perspective. Even though the people did not always see the full glory of the law nor recognize God's gracious purpose in speaking with them, there was at least one man who did. The man who was right at the heart of it all, the man who led Israel out of slavery and through the sea, that man Moses, did see the glory and beauty of the law. His heart had been touched by the grace of God so he could exclaim:

> For what great nation is there that has a god so near to it as the Lord our God is to us, whenever we call upon him? And what great nation is there, that has statutes and ordinances so righteous as all this law which I set before you this day?' (Deut. 4:7–8).

Yes, all those strange laws in the Old Testament were still good news. They did not represent God's ideal, for God was not dealing with ideal people. His great desire for them, as for us, is to be able to inscribe his law on the heart. Then we will no longer face that potential aggravation which is always lurking in the imperative. Then we can revel in the new covenant experience, an experience which enables us to live from the heart and with joy.

In the meantime, whenever I find myself chafing under the divine imperative, I find it so very helpful to retrace the steps from Sinai back to the Red Sea and there catch a fresh vision of the great God who first delivered his people and *then* brought them to Sinai. Or in terms of the New Testament, I find the sting of the imperative simply vanishing in the knowledge that while I was still his enemy, he died for me.

CHAPTER FIVE

Could you invite a Canaanite home to lunch?

'You shall be to me a kingdom of priests and a holy nation'
(Exodus 19:6).

'You shall not walk in the customs of the nation which I am casting out before you; for they did all these things, and therefore I abhorred them'

(Leviticus 20:23).

This chapter attempts to speak to a problem that is particularly acute for conservative Christians, for people of deep convictions about the life that God would have them live, for people who do not wish to contaminate the pure and holy with the filth of the world. To borrow a New Testament phrase, it seeks to deal with the problem of being in the world, but not of the world (cf. John 17: 14–18).

If you have read even a little bit of the Old Testament description of the conquest of Canaan, you will suspect that a faithful Israelite of that period would never invite a Canaanite home to lunch. As I read Joshua and Judges, I get the impression that an Israelite would have been much more inclined to invite him to a lynching, a hanging, an execution, to anything, in fact, except fellowship at a common meal. There are hints in the Pentateuch that the Lord did not intend actually to give the land of the Canaanites to Israel until the 'iniquity of the Amorites' was complete (cf. Gen. 15:16). When this iniquity was complete, the land was ready to 'vomit them out' (cf. Lev. 18:28;

20:22). The Lord was then ready to give the land to his people Israel. He warned them, however, not to share in the iniquity of their predecessors or the land would vomit them out as well (Lev. 18:24–30; 20:22–23). Small wonder that Joshua and company went about their task with such vigour. And this emphasis on separation has left its mark on both Testaments; 'peculiar', 'holy', 'separate', 'Touch not the unclean thing', 'Come out of her my people', are all well-known watch-words calling for a people apart (cf. Ex. 19:5; Deut. 14:2; 2 Cor. 6:17; Rev. 18:4).

This emphasis on distinctness and separateness for God's people leads to a two-fold problem. First, it suggests that ancient Israel was to be in almost total isolation from the evil influences in her environment. Yet Israel's history through the time of the judges and the kings clearly shows that Israel repeatedly fell into worshipping the gods of her neighbours. There is no reason to doubt that record of apostasy, but it does raise the question of Israel's relationship with Canaanite culture when she was not in apostasy, but was right with her God. Could it really be possible that Israel was one moment in splendid isolation from her neighbours, and the next moment thoroughly immersed in the surrounding evil? Such violent swings of the pendulum are quite possible, but are they realistic when we look closely at the biblical, archaeological, and historical record? That is one problem that we need to address.

The second problem touches on the implications for Christian living when one accepts the position that the people of God are to be separate and holy. Is God calling us to stand apart? Or is he asking us to mingle with the world in a life-bringing association with the world? The answer must be yes on both counts, of course, but that is hardly a solution to our problem. Perhaps a closer study of ancient Israel's relationship to her neighbours can shed light on this practical problem that continually faces the devout and serious-minded Christian living in a polluted world. In fact, I think the case is stronger than just 'perhaps', for I have been very much helped by a clearer understanding of the relationship between Israel and her neighbours. Furthermore, as we study this relationship, we can discover fascinating insights into difficult Old Testament passages.

In previous chapters we have already noted numerous points in support of the view that the Old Testament depicts a drastic accommodation on the part of God to the needs of a fallen people. The handling of the satanic figures in the Old Testament, the remarkable adjustments to culture evident in the laws possessed by ancient Israel, the way in which Israel viewed the gods of her neighbours, all suggest numerous contacts with the surrounding culture, but contacts that were in the process of being purified.

ISRAEL AND THE GODS OF CANAAN

We now need to take a closer look at several specific points that have come to light in recent decades as a result of a remarkable archaeological discovery. The name of the site in the territory of ancient Tyre which has generated so much interest is Ras Shamra, the modern name for the ancient city of Ugarit. Not only have the discoveries been fascinating for their content, but the find is remarkable, also, because the really scintillating discoveries came to light in just a matter of days after work began on the mound of Ras Shamra in 1929. Every true archaeologist tells himself that he must be willing to settle for mundane artifacts as his noble contribution to the science, but no one complains over a glorious discovery like that of Ras Shamra.

In short, Ras Shamra has opened up fresh vistas for our knowledge of ancient Canaan, its language, culture, and religion. We now know that classical biblical Hebrew is not really the language of heaven (as much as Hebrew teachers might like to think so), but it is simply the language of Canaan. The Ugaritic language is a very near relation of Hebrew and our knowledge of Hebrew has been greatly enhanced by the study of Ugaritic. But what is particularly interesting for our purposes is the knowledge of Canaanite religion and culture that Ras Shamra has bequeathed us. Among the finds were several tablets containing the myths of these ancient inhabitants of Canaan. Since these texts are dated about 1400 BC, it is not at all unreasonable to conclude that the beliefs and religious practices revealed in these tablets are fair samples of what Israel faced when she entered the land of Canaan.

One of the prominent gods in these tablets is the god Baal. In the artwork of Canaan he is often depicted with a thunderbolt and a bull, symbolizing his role as storm god and bringer of fertility. By recognizing that the bull is Baal's favourite animal, we can begin to understand the dangerous implications of the golden calf at Sinai and Jeroboam's two golden calves. The Israelites probably weren't actually worshipping Baal right then, but what were they doing with his pet bull? That was what Moses and the prophets wanted to know, too. Israel was playing with fire.

But Baal is not the only god that surfaces in the Ras Shamra texts. El, the chief god of the ethical realm, is also prominent. Elyon, the 'Most High' god, also finds a place in the Canaanite pantheon. That is not surprising in itself, since all the ancient nations had a complete pantheon of deities. The surprise comes when we turn to the Old Testament and find the names 'El' and 'Elyon' actually applied to the one true God, Yahweh. But don't jump to hasty conclusions, for there is no evidence whatsoever in the Old Testament that 'official' approval was ever granted for Israel to worship these Canaanite gods. What has happened is simply that Israel borrowed the *names* and applied them to her God, Yahweh.

A good biblical passage for illustrating this usage of several different names for the one true God is Genesis 14. According to Genesis 14:18–24, Melchizedek was priest of El Elyon (God Most High). He refers to El Elyon as the God who has delivered Abraham's enemies into his hands. Then Abraham said that he had sworn by LORD Most High (Yahweh El Elyon) not to touch the spoil (Gen. 14:24). Thus the biblical narrative clearly links all three names and applies them to the one true God. Now to borrow the names of Canaanite deities may seem like dangerous business, and perhaps it is, but the evidence from the Old Testament is quite clear. Nevertheless, we must remind ourselves again that the Old Testament is unequivocal in claiming that Israel was to worship only the one true God, Yahweh: 'You shall have no other gods before me' (Ex. 20:3). Perhaps we could illustrate the point by dramatizing a hypothetical conversation between an Israelite and a Canaanite. As the Canaanite begins to chatter away about El or Elyon, the Israelite interrupts and says: 'But do you want to know who El *really* is? He is Yahweh. And do you want to know who Elyon is? Why Yahweh, of course!'

The Bible nowhere indicates why some Canaanite names for God could be used and not others. Apparently some names were just too loaded with dangerous implications. Thus the names of several national deities such as Dagon, Chemosh and Rimmon are never used for Yahweh. But the one name that is really tantalizing is that of Baal. The prophets are vehement in their denunciations of Baal worship. Elijah, for example, took personal responsibility for killing 450 of Baal's prophets (I Kings 18:19, 40). Clearly this importation of a foreign god by Ahab's wife Jezebel, a princess of Tyre, was not to be taken lightly. Yet for all that furore against Baal, tell-tale hints suggest that at one time even the name *baal* could be used to refer to Yahweh. Probably the reason for this early usage lies in the fact that the word *baal* was originally simply an ordinary word meaning something like 'lord' or 'master'. This is probably the meaning in Hosea 2:16 where the prophet reports the words of Yahweh: 'You will call me "My Husband," and no longer will you call me, "My Baal".' In other words, when Israel is restored to God, it will be like the husband-wife relationship, not the master-slave relationship implied by the name *baal*. So the prophet is clear that the name *baal* carries with it at least a wrong theological connotation; when you are right with me, you won't want to call me 'my *baal*' (master), but rather 'my husband'.

Going back further in Israel's history, however, there is evidence to suggest that *baal* was indeed an innocent title that could be used for Yahweh. Nowhere in the Old Testament is God actually addressed as Baal, but *baal* appears in some early place and personal names. One story where this is illustrated is found in 2 Samuel 5. Once when David was fighting against the Philistines and Yahweh had given him the victory, he named the place *Baal-perazim*, saying: 'Yahweh has broken through my enemies before me, like a bursting flood.' The biblical account adds the explanation: 'Therefore the name of the place is called Baal-perazim' (2 Sam. 5:20). The RSV footnote translates the name as 'Lord of breaking through'. Apparently at this stage of Israel's history the name *baal* was not seen to be as dangerous as it was at other crisis points in history.

One other clue to the changing attitudes towards the name *Baal* is found in the names Ishbosheth and Mephibosheth. Both of these names are used in 2 Samuel to refer to the descendants of Saul (2 Sam. 3:7; 4:4), but in the genealogies of Chronicles these same names appear as Eshbaal and Meribbaal (1 Chron. 8:33–34). Comparison shows that these are precisely the same men, but the names are different. Why? One popular explanation focuses on the element *bosheth* which in Samuel apparently replaces the original element *baal* in both names. Since *bosheth* actually means 'shame' in Hebrew, many scholars have suggested that pious scribes of a later date substituted the element 'shame' in place of the hated '*baal*' to indicate to the readers the 'shameful' practice of former years: the use of the name '*baal*' among the people of Yahweh. The Chronicler probably relied on older genealogies which preserved the original names, names which, in the view of the author of Samuel, were a shameful mark on the history of Israel.

In the eyes of the faithful scribes of a later era, an era when the implications of worshipping Jezebel's god Baal were all too clear, the earlier practice appeared most shameful. But originally the attitude towards the name *baal* was neutral. Hence, even the people of God would be able to use it with no qualms of conscience. With the passage of time, however, a special threat to Israelite religion developed, and that particular bit of 'culture' had to be eliminated. That is the way God always works in relationship to culture. He will use those things that are innocent, but when they become dangerous, they must be eliminated. Even the good gifts of God can become perverted. For some, whose passions are particularly strong, certain of God's gifts may have to remain outside the limit. As for names and words, we all know of perfectly good words that have been ruined by a perverted public. Furthermore, certain words that are innocent in one culture may be quite 'loaded' in another and must be avoided if one does not wish to be misunderstood. That was apparently what happened with the name *baal*: an innocent word had been ruined.

But what was it about the god Baal that ruined the word *baal*? Here is where the Ras Shamra tablets are again most helpful, for in connection with the worship of Baal, the Canaanites had apparently developed a thoroughly degraded form of fertility worship, so degraded, in fact, that reading the ancient texts can be quite offensive to refined tastes. Baal, as the chief god of fertility, was the focal point of all their lewd rites.

To describe the matter briefly, the Canaanites believed that the fertility of the soil was a reflection of the fertility of the gods. To ensure that the rains would come to nourish growing things, sacred prostitutes, male and female, performed their orgies in the 'official' worship of the Canaanite temples. Now we can understand more clearly than ever before why Yahweh told his people not to come near the Canaanites, at least not in respect to their worship habits. The sexual drive can be a powerful force for good or for evil; the Canaanites not only used it for evil, but did so in sacred places. In our day we are, of course, accustomed to the abuse of sex in 'sinful' places. Imagine the confusion when it appeared in 'holy' places! That was the problem Israel had to face in ancient Canaan.

TWO VIEWS OF HISTORY

But having recognized the great degradation of Canaanite religion and the critical danger that it must have been to Israel, it is most helpful to look at the kinds of concessions that God made so that his people could be in the world but not of the world. To understand those concessions we need to understand something about the basic contrast between the way the Israelites looked at their history and the typical Canaanite view.

To define the difference briefly, we can say that Israel saw history as linear and goal-oriented; the Canaanites saw history as cyclical and natural. The Christian view is so heavily indebted to the Israelite way of thinking in this respect that it is easy for us to overlook how unique her outlook really was. Israel saw God dealing with his world along a time line, marked by the creative and saving acts of her God. Yahweh had created the world; he had delivered his people from Egypt; he had brought them into the land of Canaan; and Israel looked forward to the day when Yahweh would come and judge the world in righteousness (cf. Ps. 98). Christians simply added the events of the Christ event to that time-line and defined the goal more specifically as the Second Coming of Christ. We are in process, we are headed towards a goal; or to use an old gospel phrase, we are marching to Zion. Life may be good now, but the real goal of history is in the future when the full rule of God will be established.

The Canaanites, by contrast, shared the view of the vast majority of ancient civilizations: life is an unending cycle, marked by the unchanging sequence of natural events: autumn, winter, spring, summer; equinox, solstice, equinox, solstice. The more things change, the more they remain the same. History had no goal. Repetition was the key with the ever-recurring cycle of growth and decay, birth and death.

The implications of these two contrasting world-views for religious belief and practice are dramatic. Israel was called to celebrate what God had done for her in history and to anticipate his great acts of the future. Yahweh was always above history yet acting in history for his people. The Canaanites, on the other hand, saw themselves immersed in a natural world which in some strange way was virtually identical with the gods that they worshipped. The world and its inhabitants had somehow emerged from estranged bits of deity. The gods lived and died; they fought and flaunted their prowess in sexual orgies. To ensure the continuance of the natural order humans must imitate on earth what they see taking place in the heavenly realm, and that explains the prominent place of the 'sacred' sexual activity. Natural fertility, human fertility, and the fertility of the gods were all closely linked together and all three aspects dominated the worship practices of the Canaanites.

Standing as far removed from the Ugaritic civilization as we do, the implications of the religious texts are not always transparent. Still, the broad outline is clear enough. One scenario that I find particularly helpful in under-standing the Old Testament is provided by the annual death and rebirth of Baal. As in all nature religions, the religion of the Canaanites placed great importance on the movement of the heavenly bodies. The autumn and spring equinoxes, the summer and winter solstices were great festive occasions. In Palestine the regular pattern of seasons made an interesting contribution to the worship cycle, for the rains regularly came during the winter, thus preparing for the harvest of the following summer. But the summer itself was normally devoid of rain. Hence, in popular theology, Baal was said to die in the spring. Since there were no storms in the summer, the storm god must surely be dead. But in autumn, he came back to life and brought with him the abundant winter rains. To ensure this cycle, great fertility rites were enacted at the two equinoxes. Presumably, if the ritual were not right, Baal would not come back to life and there would be no winter rains, and thus no harvest the following summer.

Let's look now at a couple of Old Testament stories which suddenly come alive with meaning if the scenario suggested above is correct. First, the story of Mt. Carmel and the struggle between Baal and Yahweh. The back-ground is provided by Ahab's apostasy from Yahweh, and his active worship of Baal, the god of his wife Jezebel. The prophet of Yahweh did his best to stem the evil tide, but seemingly was quite helpless. He felt himself entirely alone in his battle, though Yahweh told him later that there were still seven thousand who had not bowed the knee to Baal (1 Kings 19:18).

Now if Ahab and his Baal-worshipping subjects had also adopted the natural theology of Baal worship, they would have been worshipping Baal and attributing to him the abundance of their flocks and fields. High treason in a land that was ruled by Yahweh! So Yahweh decided to show who was really in charge of the storms and winter rains. Elijah confronted Ahab and announced: 'As Yahweh the Elohim of Israel lives, before whom I stand, there shall be neither dew nor rain these years, except by my word' (1 Kings 17:1). With that outburst, Elijah headed for the hills. Ahab and company could cry to Baal as much as they wanted and perform all their degraded rites, but nothing would happen; and nothing did.

In the third year (1 Kings 18:1), Yahweh brought the matter to a head with a great confrontation between himself and Baal on Mt. Carmel. 'How long will you go limping between two different opinions? If Yahweh is Elohim, follow him; but if Baal, then follow him. And the people did not answer him a word' (1 Kings 18:21). Then Elijah set the stage for the test: 'You call on the name of your Elohim, and I will call on the name of Yahweh; and the Elohim who answers by fire, he is Elohim' (1 Kings 18:24). Now notice that Yahweh has touched right at the nerve of Baal worship: Baal is the storm god, the god who brings rain, the god with the fiery thunderbolt. 'We shall see,' declared Yahweh, 'who really makes it rain and who really controls the fiery thunderbolt.'

The story must be read in its entirety to feel the full thrust of Yahweh's power, but, in short, no answer came from Baal. It was Yahweh who flashed the bolt of fire and who brought the rain. If anyone in Israel had had any questions about who the real storm god was, and who it was who really made the crops grow, now it was clear. In the words of the people on Mt. Carmel: 'Yahweh, he is Elohim; Yahweh, he is Elohim' (1 Kings 18: 39).

One further glimpse into this life and death struggle between Yahweh and Baal is found in 1 Samuel 12. The context does not mention the personal deity, Baal, but rather the temptation to serve 'Baals and Ashtaroth,' two general terms to refer to the tendency to worship other gods. Nevertheless, in the light of what we now know about Canaanite religion the story is fascinating.

The background of the incident is Israel's request for a king. Samuel was deeply hurt and rather angry about the whole affair. The people's request for a king was not only a rejection of his leadership, but of the leadership of Yahweh. Fearing that a king would lead Israel away from Yahweh, Samuel decided to remind the people of Yahweh's power over the elements. The incident took place in the time of the wheat harvest, that is, in summer. No one would ever expect rain in Palestine at that time of year. The Canaanites, of course, would claim that it couldn't rain because Baal was dead. But Israel served Yahweh, a God who neither slumbers nor sleeps (cf. Ps. 121:4), to say nothing of lying dead for half the year. Yahweh could make it rain if he wished. In the words of the biblical account: 'Samuel called upon Yahweh and Yahweh sent thunder and rain that day; and all the people greatly feared Yahweh and Samuel (1 Sam. 12:18). Right in the middle of Baal's off-season, Yahweh struck a blow to show that he, Yahweh, was still lord of the land. The people were indeed terrified and in their fright almost volunteered to take back their evil request for a king (1 Sam. 12:19). Samuel admitted that their request had been evil, but he chose to let them continue in their plans for a king, reminding them that if they would remember Yahweh as their God, all would go reasonably well in spite of their wickedness (1 Sam. 12:20–25).

Both of these stories reveal Yahweh confronting the issues raised by the Canaanite thought world. They show the great threat that Baal posed to Israel's religion, but also how Yahweh could turn that very threat into a marvellous demonstration of a God who is the true master of the storm and the true overlord of all nature. Perhaps these stories should also suggest to modern Christians the great need to answer the questions that people are asking. To know those questions, we cannot cut ourselves off from culture. We must always be in the world, but never of the world.

ISRAEL'S FESTIVAL CALENDAR

Several other aspects of Israel's worship activities can shed helpful light on our struggles to remain pure, but also in touch with people and the world. One fascinating aspect is Israel's festival calendar. Often conservative Christians shy away from a liturgical calendar because of the pagan implications that are so often seen to lurk in such events as Christmas and Easter. So what was Israel doing when the Canaanites were celebrating their wild festivals? They were having their own party. God did not command abstinence from all festivals simply because the Canaanites had evil ones. Rather he gave them a festival calendar rich in the right kind of meaning. The full calendar is outlined in Leviticus 23. The details need not concern us here, but several general aspects are noteworthy.

First, at those times of the year when the Canaanites were having their most flamboyant festivals, Israel also celebrated her greatest feasts. The Passover and Firstfruits came roughly at the time of the spring equinox; the Feast of Tabernacles (also known as Booths, or Ingathering) fell at the time of the autumn equinox. Second, Israel's great feasts were fertility festivals in a sense, but in no way were they fertility orgies. Israel simply brought her firstfruits as symbols of her gratitude to the great God who had given them prosperity and health. Israel did nothing to bring about the fertility of the soil; Yahweh had already given everything as a gift. Israel could only respond in gratitude and with renewed commitment.

Third, and perhaps most important of all, the primary thrust of these two great festivals pointed to those very deeds which separated Israel so completely from her neighbours, namely, God's great saving acts in Israel's history. At the passover, Israel remembered the deliverance from Egypt; at the Feast of Tabernacles, Israel remembered the entry into the promised land, harking back to the long years of wandering when they had only temporary 'booths' or 'tabernacles'. Thus the people were led to glorify that God who had acted on their behalf, even though they did not deserve it. And though Israel's festivals recurred annually, they served as a constant reminder of that linear concept of history which began with creation and followed through all of God's great deeds for his people. At each of Israel's festivals, this praise for God's saving acts in history went hand in hand with gratitude for the fertility of the soil.

On balance, then, Israel's worship shows some concessions to the practices of the time, but only in a very limited
way. Certainly the nature of Israel's worship was radically
different from that of the Canaanites. One could perhaps
go so far as to suggest that the time (spring and autumn)
and the theme (fertility) were similar, but the use of the
time and development of the theme were worlds apart.
We have inherited much from ancient Israel, and the very
strength of the Judeo-Christian tradition points to the fact
that when it comes to the power of a pure religion, the
Canaanites and Baal were no match for Israel and Yahweh.

CONCESSIONS TO CANAANITE CULTURE

Several other interesting insights have emerged from the
study of Canaanite culture and religion. Brief mention will
suffice to illustrate the kind of concessions to culture that
God was willing to make for Israel, and can thus be of help
to us as we seek to relate to the world around us. In
particular, sacred places, sacred buildings, and sacred
hymns all have points of contact with the surrounding
culture.

The wanderings of the patriarchs and the early days of
the settlement in Israel show that a holy place often
develops a reputation which makes it attractive to a
variety of worshippers. The worshippers of Yahweh could
erect an altar to Yahweh; the worshippers of other deities
would build altars to their own gods. This same pheno-
menon is evident in Jerusalem today where holy sites are
shared by several world religions, religions that have often
been less than friendly towards each other.

Perhaps what is even more surprising for conservative
Christians is to realize that the layout of the great Israelite temples was not really unique to Israel. Rather,
they shared the same features of the Canaanite temples.
God had indeed commanded Moses to make everything
according to the pattern which he had seen in the
mountain (Ex. 25:40), but putting the archaeological evidence together with the biblical evidence, we would have to
conclude that Yahweh had simply given Moses the
pattern of a temple that Moses or anyone else would

recognize as a temple. What went on in that temple would be something quite different, but anyone walking by Israel's temple would at least be able to recognize that this was indeed a place of worship.

Sacred music is in some ways the most surprising of all the points of contact with ancient Canaan, yet when we look at centuries of Christian practice, we will have to admit that Christians have taken music and words which originated in quite diverse situations, and have moulded them into the service of faith. Apparently that is what happened in ancient Israel. In the light of the Ras Shamra texts we now know that several of our Psalms are remarkably similar to hymns to Baal. Psalms 18, 29, and 93 are some of the more notable ones. Does that mean that Israel was singing hymns to Baal? Not at all! They took hymns that described the glories of Baal and scratched out the name of 'Baal', putting in the name 'Yahweh' instead: 'Do you really want to know who is strong and mighty and shakes the mountains? It isn't Baal, it is Yahweh.' The violence and vigour of some of the psalms reflect the violence and vigour of the people who sang them. Even the style of God's revelation at Sinai was designed to meet that kind of people. You will note that the psalms that show remarkable parallels are those which extol the power and greatness of the deity, not his illicit activities, which would, of course, be abhorrent to the worshipper of Yahweh. But having said that, the evidence suggests that in certain limited ways, it was quite possible for Israel to step right in line with a Canaanite poem, strike a note higher and sing the praises of the great God of the universe. That conclusion still surprises me, but I think it has something important to say to us about the way that God deals with people.

So in conclusion, we can ask the question: when Israel was right with God, was she also in isolation from the world? Not at all! Did she compromise her faith? Yes, quite often, but only when she had turned her back on Yahweh. There was no compromise when under the guidance of Yahweh, she left those things alone which could destroy and adapted those things that she could use. And, of course, there were fresh new things that God

gave to his people, things which had no parallel anywhere. They were God's special gift to his people.

And that is also the way it must be with God's New
Testament people, his church.

CHAPTER SIX

The Worst Story in the Old Testament: Judges 19–21

In those days there was no king in Israel;
every man did what was right in his own eyes
(*Judges 21:25*).

This chapter and the next one are linked together in a couple of rather curious ways. First, they are related by way of contrast: one is the worst story, the other the best. Second, the role of the king is significant for the content of both chapters. We shall return momentarily to the role of the king, but perhaps we ought to spend at least a moment with those words 'worst' and 'best'.

How does one go about determining which story is worst and which is best? I will confess that my choices were hardly made in any scientific manner. Nevertheless, I strongly suspect that both the casual and the serious reader of the Old Testament would admit that the story in Judges 19–21 contains more blood-curdling elements than any other in the Old Testament. The discovery of the Messiah as the best story is the result of a much more thoughtful process, but that is not the case with this 'worst' story, for even a quick glance through Judges 19–21 raises a number of questions about the activities of both God and of man.

But if the story causes us problems, we can take heart from the fact that it was also a problem for the biblical writer. In fact, that appears to be at least part of the reason why the story appears in our Bible at all. So before we attempt to make some sense out of the details, we need to examine the author's attitude towards his own story. We don't actually know when it was written nor by whom. It was probably put in its present form sometime during the monarchy, apparently by someone who firmly believed that a good king was one of the greatest blessings that could happen to a land. Therein lies the clue to the author's attitude towards his story and the reason for its inclusion in Scripture.

Placing the story in its context with a brief review of Israel's history, we note that Israel had finally entered Canaan after the forty years in the wilderness. Conditions during the period of the settlement were mixed, at best, for Israel was only partially successful in driving out or subjugating the native inhabitants. Then came the judges. Just how long the period of the judges lasted is not clear from the biblical record. Although a superficial reading of the book might suggest that the judges ruled Israel one after the other in a clear chronological sequence, a closer study of the book along with an analysis of the geography of Palestine suggests that many of the judges must have ruled simultaneously, with each judge responsible for the tribes in his immediate area. In any event, stability was hardly a feature of the Israelite community during this period.

With the advent of the monarchy, stable government became at least an occasional feature of Israelite life, though not until well into the reign of David. But during the course of the monarchy the quality of leadership varied greatly, even more so after the division of the monarchy into the Kingdom of Israel (north) and the Kingdom of Judah (south). According to the biblical account, the northern kings were evil without exception; none of them ever merits a 'good' rating anywhere in the biblical record. Down south, however, the royal line was periodically brightened by a king noted for his faithfulness. Two kings who gained some of the highest marks, Hezekiah and Josiah, reigned towards the end of Judah's monarchy, so all the way through the history of the southern kingdom the occasional good king appeared who could have provided the inspiration for the author of Judges 19–21.

WHY ISRAEL NEEDED A KING

The fact that our author was a great supporter of the monarchy is not only evident in the way he tells the story, it is also crucial for its interpretation. Note what the author says right at the beginning: 'In those days, when there was no king in Israel . . .' (Judges 19:1). Then after telling the whole story, he concludes: 'In those days there was no king in Israel; every man did what was right in his own eyes' (Judges 21:25). I can almost imagine the storyteller in a summer camp setting; everyone has finished the day's activities and has snuggled down around the campfire: 'Let me tell you a story of a time when there was no king in Israel. The country went wild; everyone did his own thing. And that is precisely what happens when there is no king in the land: everyone does what is right in his own eyes.'

Thus, by linking the story with those comments about the value of kingship, the author lets us know that the heart of his story portrays a tragic tale of human wantonness and disregard for law and order. This way of interpreting the story is reinforced by the similar treatment given to the one just preceding it in Judges 17–18. There the author portrays the shocking drama of Micah and his graven image. There, also, the same commentary twice appears: 'There was no king in Israel' (Judges 17:6; 18:1). Micah had made a graven image and was worshipping it in his own way. Then the tribe of Dan came by, stealing the image to set up in their own tribal shrine. To deepen the shock further, the biblical writer notes that the chief priest in this idolatrous shrine was actually a descendant of the great Moses: 'Jonathan, the son of Gershom, the son of Moses' (Judges 17:30).

There was no king in Israel; every man did what was right in his own eyes' (Judges 17:6; 21:25). Both of these stories at the end of the book of Judges illustrate the great depravity that can pollute a land in the absence of a proper king.

By now, however, if you have grown up in a Christian context with a knowledge of the more popular Old Testament stories, this emphasis on kingship may have raised a question or two. I have discovered that if I toss out a question to a group of Christians who are quite well versed in their Old Testament, asking them whether or not kingship was a good idea for Israel, I almost invariably get the response that it was *not* a good idea. Apparently we simply remember all too well Samuel's famous response to the people when they asked for a king. He was most upset; it was a great sin to ask for a king as even the people finally admitted (see 1 Sam. 8–12). But interestingly enough, if we canvass the Old Testament as a whole for attitudes towards kingship, the only place where we find a negative evaluation is in the first part of 1 Samuel. After 1 Samuel 16 describes how the Spirit has passed from Saul to David, the negative attitude towards kingship simply disappears. Hence, we must conclude that the sin of the people did not lie in selecting kingship as a form of government, but rather in their motive when they asked for a king; namely, they simply wanted to be like the other nations (cf. 1 Sam. 8:5). Kingship itself could be a great blessing, but only when sought for the right reason.

There are a couple of other aspects in the biblical record which lend additional positive reinforcement to the idea of kingship. One lies in the glorious role assigned to the king in the psalms. Numerous examples could be cited, but perhaps the most notable one is Psalm 72, which does nothing but sing the praises of the king from beginning to end. With a hymn like that in Scripture we ought to be more cautious before we completely write off kingship as a total failure.

THE CONCEPT OF THE MESSIAH

But the most significant positive reinforcement of the idea of kingship lies in the concept of a messiah. We are so accustomed to thinking of Jesus Christ as *the* promised Messiah of Scripture, that we can easily overlook the fact that the word 'messiah' has a long and royal history. In the first instance, our English word 'messiah' is simply a transliteration of the Hebrew word *mashiaḥ*; this also comes into Greek in a transliterated form as *messias*. But the actual meaning of *mashiaḥ/messias/messiah* is 'anointed one'. That very same word is translated into Greek as *christos*. Now the interesting thing about *mashiaḥ* is that it was originally an ordinary word which could be applied to any person who was anointed. In a sense, then, it is like the words *satan* and *baal* which were also once just ordinary words. But because we now confess Jesus Christ to be *the* anointed one, it is easy to forget the ordinary background of *messiah/christos*.

A couple of references to the ordinary usage of 'messiah' might help to illustrate the point. In the long tussle between David and Saul, David had the opportunity on several occasions to destroy Saul, but he refused to do so: 'Yahweh forbid that I should do this thing to my lord, Yahweh's anointed (*mashiaḥ messiah*)' (1 Sam 24:6). If you were reading this same passage in Greek you would be reading about Yahweh's *christ(os)*. And who is the *christ(os)* in this instance? None other than the king, the very human Saul. This application of 'anointed one' to the king is also a frequent feature of the psalms (e.g. Ps. 2:2; 18:50; 20:6). The 'anointed one' in the Old Testament is usually the king, though the word itself could apply to anyone who had been anointed. As the history of Israel progressed, the people began to look for the ideal king of the future, *the* anointed one *par excellence*. That, of course, was when the word could begin to appear as Messiah, with a capital M. When Jesus' followers accepted him as *the* Messiah, the word was no longer an ordinary one; it now referred to that specific fulfilment of the ancient hope of God's people. But that is transgressing on the theme of our next chapter, so we must return to Judges 19–21.

I have deliberately taken considerable care in establishing the fact that the idea of kingship could be viewed positively in Israel. Samuel's speeches have had such a powerful impact on Christian tradition that an important truth has almost been obscured. And, of course, the most important piece of evidence for tempering our criticism of kingship lies in the fact that Jesus Christ himself claimed to stand in that royal line of David. That should guard us from supporting too loudly the position which Samuel took. He was so appalled at the people's motive, that his speech spilled over into what has been interpreted as a general condemnation of kingship. The rest of the biblical tradition is necessary to balance the picture.

Returning then to Judges 19–21, we discover that the author of these stories is a wholehearted supporter of the 'low road' approach to interpreting Israel's history. He stands on a vantage point and is looking back at a frightful piece of his own heritage. Actually, both this story and the one preceding it are some of the best examples for establishing the validity of the 'low road' approach to the Old Testament. I have noted with interest that Christian writers who work primarily with the 'high road' approach often make no attempt whatsoever to interpret these stories. When we emphasize the greatness of Israel's faith and the nobility of her heroes, it is hard to believe that things could really get as bad as they did. But they were bad, very bad, and that we shall see as we turn now to the story itself.

KEY FEATURES

If you haven't already read the story through, noting the key features and the problems, I would suggest that you turn to the last three chapters of Judges and do so, for then the following discussion will be much more meaningful. But in any event, I will summarize the key aspects of the story as the basis for our discussion.

The story begins with a certain Levite from the north country of Ephraim setting out to reclaim his wandering concubine from her home town of Bethlehem in Judah. His father-in-law had managed to prolong the visit by a great show of hospitality, but after several days of festivity, the party set out for home.

As evening approached, they began to look for a place to stay. Being reluctant to entrust themselves to the non-Israelite inhabitants of Jebus (Jerusalem), they went on until they came to Gibeah in Benjamin. Even here, however, no one showed them any hospitality until another Ephraimite, one who had taken up temporary residence in Gibeah, came along and urged them to stay with him. It simply wasn't safe to stay all night in the town square.

After settling in for the evening, they began to make merry. Suddenly the house was surrounded by a noisy crowd of Benjamites who were clamouring for the stranger. 'That we may know him', was the polite biblical way of referring to sexual activity, and in this instance, it was clearly homosexual activity. The host was appalled and offered his virgin daughter and the man's concubine as substitutes. When the mob remained undeterred, the Levite himself thrust out his concubine and slammed the door.

The mob poured out all their illicit passion on the poor concubine, but the Levite lifted not a finger in her behalf. In the morning he opened the door and announced to the prostrate figure on the doorstep that they should be up and going. Receiving no response, he loaded the body onto his donkey and headed for home where he proceeded to divide the corpse into twelve pieces. These he posted to all parts of the land of Israel.

Communities throughout the land were incensed and the people of Israel massed for war against Benjamin. The Benjamites, too, had got the news. They also mustered their men for war, not in alliance with Israel, but in resistance. With the two rival armies now glowering at each other, Israel demanded that the vile men be handed over. When Benjamin refused, Israel sought guidance from Yahweh about who should go up to battle first. 'Judah,' was the divine response, and the battle was joined. But what a victorious slaughter by the Benjamites! Bewildered, Israel again massed for battle and asked Yahweh if they should still go up against their brethren the Benjamites. 'Go,' was the divine response and Israel went. But again Benjamin stormed to victory.

The original convocation of the tribes had been at Mizpah, but now all the people and the army trekked to Bethel and yet again implored Yahweh for guidance: 'Should we again go up against Benjamin?' 'Go up; for tomorrow I will give them into your hand.' True enough, for this time the tables were turned and precious few of the Benjamites remained alive at the end of the day, in fact, only six hundred warriors, and these had fled to the wilderness.

But now that the people had avenged the evil, pangs of regret began to afflict them. 'Why is it, Lord,' they cried, 'that today there is lacking one tribe in Israel?' And they were faced with an even greater problem, for in their previous wrath they had sworn not to give wives to the Benjamites. Now that there were only six hundred Benjamites left, and all of these male, how could the tribe survive and grow? Canaanite wives were out of the question.

The solution lay in another oath that Israel had taken in the days of her wrath: whoever did not answer the call to arms against Benjamin would be killed. Was there any such community? Yes, Jabesh–Gilead. An army was dispatched and the entire city was massacred, except for the virgins, four hundred of them. As a gracious gesture of reconciliation these were given as wives to the Benjamites, but there still weren't enough virgins to go around. Where could one find two hundred more without breaking the oath?

'There is a yearly feast of Yahweh at Shiloh. When the maidens go out to dance in the vineyards, let each man lie in wait and seize a wife. If the brothers or fathers complain, just send them to us; we will calm them down, for without breaking our oath, each man will have received a wife.'

'In those days there was no king in Israel; every man did what was right in his own eyes.'

PROBLEMS

You have undoubtedly made your own mental list of problems as you worked through this story and your list is probably very much like mine. The wickedness of the Benjamites is clear enough, yet that is not really the same kind of problem as the others for even the Israelites of that day were unanimous in condemning the foul passion of those wicked men. The real problems lie in those aspects of the story that are *not* condemned, the aspects that are cheerfully accepted as part of the normal customs of the day. First, the ghastly double standard in hospitality offends our sense of justice. The man was carefully guarded, but daughter, female guest, and concubine could be willingly sacrificed to protect the male. Hospitality is a marvellous idea, but let us be consistent! Second, must one really send out a chunk of human flesh as a means of seeking redress? Third, and perhaps most crucial, Yahweh twice told the people to go up to battle and Israel was slaughtered for her 'obedience'. Fourth, Israel wreaked such incredible vengeance on Benjamin when Yahweh finally did give victory. Was such bloodshed really justified? Fifth, and finally, Israel made such drastic and rigid oaths, oaths which led to such frightful consequences on the one hand and such curious means of avoidance on the other.

In the discussion that follows, we shall touch on the above problems directly or indirectly. The biblical author really gives us no direct clue as to how we can resolve them. He was appalled at the Benjamite wickedness and perhaps even by their stubborn and disastrous refusal to hand over the culprits, but for answers to our other questions, we must turn elsewhere.

TRIBAL CONSCIOUSNESS AND CORPORATE PERSONALITY

Probably the biggest problem in our attempts to understand this story lies in the great gulf between our twentieth century 'Christian' culture and that in which the biblical events took place. In that connection, I have found that recognizing the implication of tribal consciousness is an important first step in our attempts to gain understanding.

In recent decades a concept has been articulated which has proved most helpful in illuminating a number of problem aspects in the Old Testament. The technical name for this concept is 'corporate personality.' It refers to the belief that a person's 'personality' extends beyond himself in both time and space. 'Personality' in this sense refers to a certain vital 'essence' which is the heart of a person's existence. This 'personality' extends in space, in that it reaches beyond the individual to include members of one's family, tribe, or nation. It extends in time, in that the impact of this person's 'personality' continues even after the person is dead.

Now Westerners, and especially Americans, have been so deeply influenced by individualist thinking, that we have great difficulty in grasping this corporate view of things. We hold it as a fundamental principle of justice that each person lives and dies on the basis of his own merits or sins. This fundamental principle is, of course, evident in Scripture as well. Abraham thought it wholly unjust that the innocent in Sodom should perish with the guilty (Gen. 18:23–25). Yet even in this conversation the corporate view lingers, for both Abraham and Yahweh assume that a minimum of ten righteous souls could save the corporate body. Ezekiel 18 is another well-known biblical passage emphasizing individual responsibility. In fact, Ezekiel seems to be combating that very tendency towards fatalism which a 'tribal' or 'corporate' view can so easily engender. Ezekiel is writing during Israel's exile in Babylon at a time when the exiles were inclined to think that 'the fathers have eaten sour grapes and the children's teeth have been set on edge' (Ezek. 18:2). In other words, thy believed that the fathers' sins had doomed the children, a clear reflection of the corporate view. Ezekiel's emphasis on individualism came, of course, several centuries after the events described in Judges 19–21, and Israel's national situation perhaps allowed an emphasis on individualism which would not have been possible previously. But having said that, we must recognize that the corporate view of life dominates the Old Testament scene and is particularly reflected in many early narratives. Perhaps a couple of illustrations would be helpful before we return to the specific discussion of the problems in Judges 19–21.

One of the more difficult stories in the Old Testament (in some ways a close relative of Judges 19–21) is found in 2 Samuel 21. The story describes how a famine had come upon Israel, persisting for three years. The reigning monarch, King David, inquired of Yahweh and was told that there was bloodguilt on Saul and his house because Saul had put the Gibeonites to death. Now Saul was dead, but the effects of his 'personality' lingered on. As king, his decisions had involved the whole nation, so, in a sense, the results of his sins affected the nation, leading, in this instance, to a famine. Only the actions of another king whose 'personality' again included all his people, could right the wrong.

But why would the great God in heaven stoop to work within a system of justice that is determined by such curious views? First, those views were not at all curious for those people; they were the norm. Second, God could not suddenly impose an individualist view on those who thought in a corporate or collective manner any more than he can suddenly impose a corporate view on those who think as individualists. At least a freedom-loving God would not seek to impose such alien norms. Furthermore, Yahweh was out to win the hearts of his people then just as much as he is out to win our hearts today. And just as he accommodates himself to us, so he was seeking to reach Israel in a way that she could appreciate. That meant accepting, at least in part, their standards of justice. We have already discussed this principle in connection with law in Scripture, so perhaps we have stressed the point enough, yet the mishandling of the Old Testament even in our own age testifies to the fact that it has not been sufficiently emphasized.

Two other aspects of the account in 2 Samuel 21 are significant for interpreting the story: the breaking and keeping of oaths, and burial rites for kings and other royalty. We shall return in another connection to the matter of oaths, but let us note briefly here how the corporate aspect relates to the material remains of deceased royalty.

When Yahweh put his finger on Saul's sin against the Gibeonites, David asked the Gibeonites how they wished the wrong to be righted. 'We simply want to hang up seven of Saul's descendants before Yahweh at Gibeon' (2 Sam. 21:6). David complied: 'The seven of them perished together' (2 Sam. 21:9). The next act in the drama seems particularly strange to us; one of Saul's concubines spread out sackcloth for herself on a rock, keeping the birds and the beasts away. When David was told, he immediately set out to provide a proper burial for the deceased members of Saul's family. What was a proper burial? Bringing the bones of the deceased back to their ancestral burial ground. So David took the bones from the men of Jabesh Gilead and the bones of the seven men who had been hanged and buried them all in the tomb of Kish, Saul's father. 'After that God heeded supplications for the land' (2 Sam. 21:14).

God worked very carefully within the parameters of justice as those people understood them. In fact, this must have been one of the major reasons why the biblical writer recorded this story, namely, to show that Yahweh is the great guarantor of justice, even bringing a famine upon the land to awaken the king and his people to those principles which the people themselves held to be binding. And for those people, both the decisions and the bones of a dead king were still something to be reckoned with. Thus we have one of the clearest examples of how 'corporate personality' affected both the everyday life of the people and the course of Israel's history.

Another story which can serve to illustrate the effect of corporate thinking in Israel is the story of Achan in Joshua 7. Achan had stolen some of the sacred booty from Jericho, and even though he was a 'small' man in Israel, the corporate or collective view of things required that the entire army of Israel suffer defeat at Ai. Achan's 'personality' had extended in a damaging way towards his fellows. That particular aspect of the story, illustrating the impact of corporate thinking, is one which most of us could probably accept, for even given our individualistic way of thinking, we know that any community and especially a Christian one, can be really successful only when it moves and acts with 'one accord' (cf. Acts 1:14). But what is even more helpful for our understanding of this story is to recognize how the corporate view is reflected in the matter of the penalty which fell on Achan and his family, especially his family, for that is the difficult aspect for us. The biblical account records that not only was Achan put to death, but everything connected with him was annihilated: the silver, the robe, the bar of gold; the sons and daughters; his oxen, asses, and sheep; his tent and all that he had (Joshua 7:24). In our day, I suspect we would hasten to sell the goods, even perhaps holding a church sale, so that this wealth, tainted though it was, would result in at lest some 'blessing to mankind'. But that was not an option in ancient Israel, for Achan's sin had touched all that was his. It was not necessary to inquire whether or not the sons, the daughters, the sheep or the tent were 'guilty'. That would be our individualist approach. In their view, Achan's sin had touched the whole community of Israel, so his penalty must touch all that was his.

Thus by recognizing how much the customs of the day permeate the biblical account, we no longer need to 'blame' God for perpetrating such harsh, cruel, and unjust punishments. Judged by Israel's standards, Joshua had lived by both the letter and the spirit of justice when he commanded in the name of Yahweh that Achan and his family be destroyed. For Yahweh to have commanded anything different at that point in time would have been seen as grossly unjust, and would have raised the question in the minds of thoughtful Israelites as to whether or not Yahweh really knew what justice was all about, and hence if he were really worthy to be God in Israel. But Yahweh knew his people and acted accordingly. It is our responsibility to understand them so that we can more clearly understand him.

I hope this glimpse of Israel's tribal consciousness, her corporate way of thinking, will help explain why the family affair in Judges 19–21 was such an intense scene. In spite of her many quarrels, Israel knew that the tribes belonged together. The people were heartbroken when they faced the stark possibility that one of the twelve could disappear (cf. Judges 21:3, 15). But now let us look at the specific customs which are part of the story, customs which were quite normal in Israel, but which are a great perplexity to us.

CUSTOMS THAT PERPLEX US

1. *Hospitality*

Yes, the Old Testament clearly bears witness to a male chauvinistic attitude, and for much of the time this attitude seems distressingly typical and socially acceptable. Although Genesis 1 states that both male and female were made in the image of God (Gen. 1:27), Genesis 3 describes the tragic result of sin: the stronger inevitably dominates the weaker (cf. Gen. 3:16). Conservative Christians have often appealed to this verse in an attempt to demonstrate that male lordship has the divine stamp of approval. But why should the 'natural' results of sin suddenly become the ideal? The New Testament clearly calls us to strive for equality between the sexes (cf. Gal. 3:28), and the Old Testament certainly contains the principles pointing in that direction. Nevertheless, the fact remains that Old Testament society, and in fact, Old Testament saints, often fell far short of the ideal. We can castigate the actors in the drama of Judges 19–21, but Lot acted in exactly the same way when the heavenly messengers arrived in Sodom; he offered his two virgin daughters so that his male guests might remain unmolested. Yet Lot was 'worthy' to be saved from the city (see Genesis 19). So here is a clear sign of the low road; Old Testament society still had a long way to go.

2. *A Piece of Flesh as an Invitation to Justice*

Nowhere else in Scripture is there even a hint that one could or should use pieces of the human body as a rallying cry for justice. I suspect that even Old Testament society cringed at this act; such may in fact, have been the major thrust of the comment in Judges 19:30: 'Such a thing has never happened or been seen from the day that the people of Israel came up out of the land of Egypt until this day; consider, take counsel, and speak.' There is, however, a later incident when Saul summoned the people to battle by sending out pieces of his yoke of oxen (see 1 Sam. 11:7).

We can conclude, therefore, that Old Testament man was not particularly squeamish at the sight of a little flesh and blood. Even so, the act here in Judges 19–21 must have been seen as particularly callous.

3. *Rigid but Avoidable Oaths*

I am certain that people today do not take oaths seriously enough. Maybe that is part of the reason why we react so strongly against the way that Old Testament society related to oaths and oath-taking. In Judges 19–21, two oaths are prominent and Israel took them very seriously indeed. The people had vowed, first, that whoever did not answer the call to arms must die, and second, that they would not give their daughters to Benjamin for wives. When the implications of the second oath began to dawn on them, they realized that their oath could lead to the disappearance of the tribe of Benjamin. In their newly-found remorse, they cast about for a way of escape. Then they realized that their other oath was just what they needed. Was there anyone who had not come to battle? Yes, the men of Jabesh-Gilead had sent no one. Following the rules of the *ḥerem* (see below), they massacred the town, saving only the virgins. But that still didn't provide enough wives for the Benjamites. Rather than admit the rashness of their oath, they chose another way of getting around it, instructing the Benjamites to take their wives by force from among the dancers at Shiloh. In this way they felt they could avoid the strictures of the oath. They couldn't actually break their oath, but they could find a way of avoiding its primary thrust.

But before we synthesize some elements in reaction to this early Israelite use of oaths, we should note a couple of other examples by way of emphasizing how deeply Israel felt the obligation of a sworn oath. We have already mentioned 2 Samuel 21 as a passage where the oath figures prominently. The famine had come upon the land because Saul had broken Israel's oath to the Gibeonites. Since Gibeon had gained the oath by deceit, the ordinary Israelite had been quite of a mind to take vengeance. But

Joshua 9:16–21 indicates that the leaders took a firm stand for the inviolability of an oath even though it had been wrongfully gained. Now Saul had broken that oath, so the land must pay the price. To put things right, the Gibeonites demanded that David hand over seven sons of Saul. David's response to that request further illustrates the sanctity of an oath, for he spared Mephibosheth the son of Jonathan, 'because of the oath of Yahweh which was between them' (2 Sam. 21:7; cf. 1 Sam. 20:17). Obviously the oath did play a significant role in Israelite life.

One other example of a rash oath is Jephthah's promise to sacrifice the first thing that came out of his house if Yahweh would grant him victory over his enemies. Jephthah was shocked and saddened when his only daughter came out first (Judges 11:34–35), but 'he did with her according to his vow which he had made' (Judges 11:39). In Israel, an oath was an oath was an oath.

Now in the light of this rigid adherence to the letter of an oath, there are two questions that we must ask: first, how are we to view God's reaction to such a state of affairs, and second, what effect should these examples have on our own use of oaths?

In response to the first question, we must admit that God clearly worked within the accepted oath-making framework of ancient Israel and I think we can understand why. Given the state of morality that is evident in Judges 19–21, God had almost nothing positive to work with as he looked at his people. So even though attitudes towards hospitality were horribly imbalanced in favour of the male, and even though the people held tenaciously to the letter of an oath with virtually no overt concern for the spirit, these conditions do provide evidence that Israel was capable of standing for something. At a time of deep depravity, that was important. In the Israelite attitude towards oaths we have a glimmer of integrity, a slender thread out of which God could begin to weave a garment of righteousness and justice. God had to begin with the raw materials that were ready to hand. As much as he and we might desire a more noble race, such does not come about by wishful thinking. In the work of character development, one can at least *begin* to work with a person who stands for something, even though he may be too rigorous and may even be standing for the wrong thing.

In this connection it might be well to reflect on the ways of growing children who are tossed a glorious conditional promise by a hopeful parent: 'We will all go to the zoo if we get the garden weeded and the music practice done.' But how easy it is for children to remember the promise and to forget the conditions. Children can recognize a promise, just as Israel could recognize an oath, but the ability to weigh conditions and contingencies is a gift that comes with maturity. In Israel at the time of the judges, that maturity was somewhat less than prominent.

So how are we to relate to oaths? In the first instance, we could all heartily agree with the admonition in Ecclesiastes 5:5 that it would be better not to vow at all than to vow and not pay. That still gives us no clue, however, as to what we are to do when a rash vow threatens to destroy innocent victims. But perhaps right there in the term 'innocent' is the answer to the problem, for surely a mature understanding of scriptural principles would lead me to conclude that I must never inflict damage or harm on an *innocent* person. To destroy that cardinal doctrine of justice for the sake of my rashness would be unthinkable, unchristian, and wrong. It must be said, however, that no consideration of personal gain should lead me to revoke an oath, and that may be just where I am most inclined to fall—I promise to sell a piece of junk around the house, only to learn that it is a valuable antique—yet that is precisely the point where a vow should hold. In the end, I must weigh my oaths against the law of God. In the interest of my supposed personal integrity, I must never sacrifice the higher law of God to my selfish oath. Rather, I must ever be willing to submit all my acts and decisions to God himself even if that means painful and embarrassing backtracking. I believe that God always expects me to do the right thing, oath or no oath, an expectation that can be fulfilled only when I am in constant touch with him.

Now I must admit that probably not many in ancient Israel would have seen any light in this general decision-making procedure that I have outlined above. But should we expect them to? To overturn specific oaths and commands on the basis of the higher principles of love, justice, and mercy, requires a level of maturity which had not yet been reached in Israel. Judges 19–21 shows that the people had come far enough to be able to recognize the disastrous effects of a rash oath, but they were not yet capable of rationalizing a way of escape that would meet the demands of consistency. In this instance they managed to squirm free of their oath by suggesting the wife-snatching escapade in the vineyards. A more sophisticated approach to ethics would have to come later. To borrow some well-known New Testament words: 'When I was a child, I spoke like a child, I thought like a child, I reasoned like a child; when I became a man, I gave up childish ways' (1 Cor. 13:11). In a sense, Israel was a child and the childish ways were still much in evidence. Interestingly enough, this imagery of the child is vividly reinforced by the moving words of the prophet Hosea:

> When Israel was a child, I loved him,
>   and out of Egypt I called my son.
> The more I called them, the more they went from me;
> they kept sacrificing to the Baals, and burning incense to idols.
> Yet it was I who taught Ephraim to walk,
>   I took them up in my arms;
>   but they did not know that I healed them.
>
> I led them with cords of compassion, with the bands of love
> and I became to them as one who eases the yoke on their jaws, and
> I bent down to them and fed them. (Hosea 11:1–4)

A 'high road' approach to the Old Testament can easily obscure this level of 'childhood' in ancient Israel. In the history of Christianity, such an 'oversight' has led to two quite different but equally unfortunate results. On the one hand, it has led to unbelief and rejection of the Old Testament as the Word of God because this earlier revelation of God seems to fall short of our 'higher' standards. On the other hand, it has led to tragic perpetuation of crude customs and immature attitudes when Christians have appealed to the Old Testament to justify an oppressive status quo. For examples, we can simply cite the use of Scripture in the nineteenth century to support slavery, and in the twentieth, to support the doctrine of male superiority.

4. Ḥerem (*devotion to destruction*)

Even if you don't know Hebrew, if you have read Judges 19–21, *ḥerem* has already offended, or at least it should have done. The word is very difficult to translate into English, and that makes the matter all the more frustrating since both the noun and verb forms appear quite often in our Old Testament. In Judges 19–21, it is directly linked with the oath to kill anyone who did not come out to war against Benjamin. When the tribes sent their warriors against Jabesh-Gilead, they instructed them to 'utterly destroy' everything except the virgins (Judges 21:11). Here 'utterly destroy' illustrates the verbal usage; the phrase 'devoted things' in the story of Achan illustrates the noun usage; i.e. Achan had taken some of the 'devoted things' from Jericho (Josh. 7:1). Actually, reading Joshua's instructions concerning the attack on Jericho (Josh. 6:15–21) can provide a fairly good feel for the use of both noun and verb. In short, *ḥerem* refers to a sacred vow, devoting something to destruction, and usually it was a whole town.

In this 'devotion', however, certain objects or persons could be saved from destruction, being 'devoted' instead to some special use. For example, Joshua declared that from Jericho, all the silver and gold along with the vessels of bronze and iron were to be reserved for sacred use: 'They shall go into the treasury of Yahweh' (Josh. 6:19). In Judges 21, the virgins of Jabesh-Gilead were 'devoted' to the purpose of providing wives for the Benjamites, but everything else, including all married women and the children, was destroyed by the sword (cf. Judges 21:10). One could not, however, randomly 'devote' people or things to some exceptional use, a lesson which becomes painfully clear in the story of Saul's attack on the Amalekites. The command of God was to 'utterly destroy' the Amalekites (1 Sam. 15:18), but Saul did not obey, lamely attempting to explain his fault by claiming that the people had saved some of the best of the flocks to sacrifice to Yahweh (1 Sam. 15:21). The rules of *herem* could include sacred exceptions as the preceding examples show, but such exceptions could not be determined at the whim of a disobedient king.

Breaking the rules of *herem* could lead to disastrous results. In Achan's case, it led first to the defeat of Israel at Ai and then to the annihilation of Achan himself, his family, and all his property. In Saul's case, transgression of the rules of *herem* resulted in his rejection as king. 'To obey is better than sacrifice' is the famous admonition, and it occurs in the context of Saul's breaking of the rules of *herem* (1 Sam. 15:22).

The concept of *herem* also appears in the Pentateuchal law code where it is applied for purely religious purposes: if anyone is reported to have seduced an Israelite city into following gods other than Yahweh, the matter shall be thoroughly investigated. If the accusation could be proved true, the entire city was to be 'devoted to destruction', including the cattle and all the spoil (Deut. 13:12–18). Rather tough words for a freedom-loving God, are they not? Yes, but Israel expected just that kind of language and just that kind of action from her God. In Israel, the religious realm could not be neatly separated from secular life. The penalties for religious offences were uniformly as rigorous as the penalties for civil misdeeds. Yahweh was over all and was responsible for maintaining justice.

In this connection, there may appear to be at least a grain of truth in that traditional appeal to 'theocracy' as a means of explaining some of the violent aspects of the Old Testament such as mass slaughter in war and the frequent use of the death penalty. That way of attempting to solve the 'problem' of the Old Testament has been very popular in conservative circles, but the 'problem' with it lies in the implied assumption that the closer one comes to direct divine rule, the more violent the treatment one can expect from the hand of God. That I simply cannot accept. Israel was directly under divine rule, but the violence of the Old Testament stems in the first instance from the human rather than from the divine.

The theocracy argument is further weakened in view of

the fact that every ancient nation was essentially a 'theocracy'. The major difference between Israel and her neighbours was not theocracy, but rather that Israel's one God was dependable. You could trust Yahweh to establish justice. In the polytheistic religions of the other nations, however, you could never be quite sure whom you could trust, for the gods were often at war with each other as well as with man. But in spite of the considerable contrast between Israel's view of theocracy and that of her neighbours, the one common feature among all the nations of the ancient world was that punishment was rigorous and it came with divine sanction. That was precisely the situation in Israel.

Looking more specifically at the frightful custom of *herem*, we have clear archaeological evidence that this custom was commonplace among Israel's neighbours. The famous Moabite stone contains the evidence for this helpful correlation. This stone bears an inscription from the Moabite king Mesha, roughly a contemporary of King Ahab of Israel. In the inscription, Mesha describes how his god Chemosh had punished the Moabites by handing them over to oppression by Israel. In gratitude to Chemosh for finally giving Moab its freedom, Mesha mentions that he had 'devoted' to destruction several Israelite cities. Here, then, is precisely the same use of *herem* as we have found in Israel, but this time with reference to Chemosh instead of to Yahweh.

I think we can safely conclude, therefore, that *herem* was not God's idea, but rather that it was a custom so deeply engrained that God not only had to tolerate it, but actively to retain it. If we see God giving laws and guidance directly from heaven with no regard for human culture, a position that has all too often been assumed by conservative Christians, then these Old Testament laws and customs are clearly incredible and testify to a God quite different from the God revealed in Jesus Christ.

Admittedly my interpretation of these customs and stories is strongly coloured by my knowledge of God as revealed in Jesus Christ. If in the gospels I find evidence of a life-giving and patient God, a God who decries any kind of coercion, a God who is the friend of sinners, then with that knowledge I am bound to return to the Old Testament and look for that same kind of God, for the New Testament clearly claims a continuity between Yahweh of the Old Testament and the God made known in Jesus Christ. Knowing what we do now about the ancient Near East and accepting the New Testament testimony about the one God, we cannot avoid this conclusion: the God of the Old Testament was extremely patient and quite willing to risk his reputation so that he could meet his people where they were. This God of the Old Testament was rough only insofar as he was dealing with rough people. But because the people were so very rough, God's actions have sometimes been misunderstood, and nowhere is that more likely to happen than in the gruesome story of Judges 19–21. If, however, we bring to the story a knowledge of a patient and freedom-loving God who will not coerce his people then this event can tell a remarkably positive story about Yahweh himself and his manner of dealing with man. Let us look, then, at the way God himself figures in this worst of all stories and see if we can better understand his ways with man.

YAHWEH'S ACTIVITY IN THE STORY

We must note in the first instance, that, in spite of the fiery passions of the Israelites and the Benjamites, the writer of the story still sees the events as under the control of Yahweh. For example, when Benjamin was finally defeated, it was Yahweh who defeated Benjamin before Israel (Judges 20:35). Even the breach between Benjamin and the other tribes was attributed to Yahweh (Judges 21:15). So we do have an awareness of Yahweh's activity in the story even though every man was doing what was right in his own eyes. But, as noted before, the biblical writers often describe Yahweh as *causing* an event when we would be more inclined to describe him as *permitting* it. Certainly the latter approach makes it possible to lay the blame for destructive acts more directly at the foot of perverted demonic and human wills. That is where I think it belongs. Israel, however, seldom saw it that way for Yahweh was all in all:

> I am Yahweh and there is no other.
> I form light and create darkness,
> I make weal and create woe,
> I am Yahweh, who do all these things. (Isaiah 45:7)

But let us come right to the heart of Yahweh's activities in Judges 19–21. Why did he twice send Israel up simply to be defeated? It is one thing to defeat the wicked Benjamites, but to let the 'righteous' suffer is quite intolerable. How can we remove this question mark about God's ways with man?

The answer lies, quite surprisingly, simply in a careful reading of the story. Let us note just what happened.

When the tribes got the message, they came together in great anger and massed for battle against Benjamin. Judges 20:11 says that all Israel massed against the city of Gibeah 'as one man'. It was then that they asked for the culprits to be handed over. Is there any wonder that Benjamin got defensive? Force begets force and Israel had thrown all her might against Gibeah *before* she tried diplomacy. What is even more remarkable is that Israel inquired of Yahweh *after* they had already massed for battle. Even then she did not ask *whether* to go to battle or not, but rather *which* of the tribes should go up *first* to battle against Benjamin (Judges 20:18).

Have you ever tried to stop a riot after it is well under way? I have been privileged to observe only very minor 'riots' (on the campus of a Christian college, no less), but even very mild riots are virtually impossible to reverse. On a college campus, to send the gentlemen back to their rooms with emotions still boiling is asking for all kinds of disaster. That is what I see happening in God's dealings with Israel, for Israel was in no position to listen to reason. Some things have to be learned the hard way. Even deserved vengeance must never be meted out with angry passion. That was the lesson that Israel had to learn.

It is also interesting to note in this connection that Yahweh instructed that Judah should go up first, Judah, the native tribe of the murdered woman, where passion for the deceased and hostility against the culprits undoubtedly burned most fiercely. Theirs was the lesson hardest to learn, so Judah went up first and took the brunt of the Benjamite victory.

Immediately following her defeat, the people 'took courage, and again formed the battle line in the same place where they had formed it on the first day' (Judges 20:22). Passion still burned hot and Israel was still itching for vengeance. But again she massed for war *first* and *then* asked Yahweh. Had the people done it the other way around the results might have been different. Israel had not yet learned her lesson and again she was defeated.

Finally, after two shattering defeats, all Israel went to Bethel and wept before Yahweh. This time they did not mass for battle and this time Yahweh said: 'Go up, for tomorrow I will give them into your hand' (Judges 20:28). The victory was won with considerable shedding of blood, but this time, with Israel's spirit headed in the right direction, Yahweh could afford to give her the victory.

How many times does God have a blessing that he longs to give to his people, but he cannot, for they have not truly turned to him? That is a significant lesson that we can learn from this worst of all stories, even if we are horrified by virtually everything else that took place.

The worst story in the Old Testament: a testimony to a great degradation among God's people, but a testimony to the great patience of a God who had not turned his back on them. He was willing to work with them through all their vicious customs, seeking to draw them to higher ground. The author of the story already stood on vantage ground, for he saw that a king could be a great benefit to the land. But we stand on even higher ground for we can see more clearly than the Old Testament man ever could, the great King himself, the great ideal of whom every Old Testament king was but a mere shadow. But that is the story that comes next, the best story in the Old Testament.

CHAPTER SEVEN

The Best Story in the Old Testament: the Messiah

The people who walked in darkness have seen a great light . . .
For to us a child is born, to us a son is given . . .

(Isaiah 9:2, 6).

My choice of best story in the Old Testament is not a specific episode like the worst story, but rather a great theme which springs from deep roots in the Old Testament and finally bursts into bloom in the New. Certainly one of the most insistent and obvious claims of the New Testament is that Jesus of Nazareth came as the fulfilment of the Old Testament messianic hope. John has recorded how Jesus chided his Jewish hearers: 'If you believed Moses, you would believe me, for he wrote of me' (John 5:46). And after the resurrection, Jesus expounded to the disciples on the Emmaus road the *real* meaning of the Old Testament: 'And beginning with Moses and all the prophets, he interpreted to them in all the scriptures the things concerning himself' (Luke 24:27). Not too long afterwards he appeared to the eleven disciples and said: 'These are my words which I spoke to you, while I was still with you, that everything written about me in the law of Moses and the prophets and the psalms must be fulfilled. Then he opened their minds to understand the scriptures' (Luke 24:44–45).

So the claim of the New Testament seems to be clear enough, but having said that, a couple of interesting and potentially distressing observations must not be overlooked. First, the Jewish community as a whole has not accepted Jesus of Nazareth as the fulfilment of the Old Testament hope. From the Jewish point of view, Christianity is a breakaway movement which has pinned its hopes on a messianic pretender. Never mind the fact that the Christian movement has been reasonably popular and successful; the point is that Judaism has rejected the claim of the New Testament that Jesus is the fulfilment of the Old Testament messianic hope.

The second observation that we must not neglect is that Jesus' own disciples so radically misunderstood his mission. The synoptic gospels, Matthew, Mark and Luke, in particular, highlight the contrast between Jesus' grasp of his mission and that of his disciples. Nowhere is this more clearly demonstrated than in Matthew 16 where Peter openly proclaims to Jesus: 'You are the Christ (Messiah), the Son of the living God' (Matt. 16:16). Jesus was pleased with Simon's confession, though he warned the disciples that the time was not yet ripe to share this conviction (Matt. 16:20). Then he opened to them the real nature of his mission: 'From that time Jesus began to show his disciples that he must go to Jerusalem and suffer many things from the elders and chief priests and scribes, and be killed, and on the third day be raised' (Matt. 16:21). Peter's response? 'God forbid, Lord! This shall never happen to you.' To which Jesus replied: 'Get behind me, Satan! You are a hindrance to me; for you are not on the side of God, but of men' (Matt. 16:23).

Now one might think that conversations like that should have been clear enough, yet apparently the disciples either could not or would not believe. Returning to Luke's description of the Emmaus Road conversation, we learn that the followers of Jesus were stunned and disheartened by Jesus' death; 'We had hoped that he was the one to redeem Israel' (Luke 24:21). To be sure, after Jesus had appeared several times to the disciples following the resurrection, they caught a fresh vision of their risen Lord, a vision both in the physical and spiritual sense, and the book of Acts records the powerful impact of that post-resurrection experience. So the disciples finally did believe, no question about that, but the point I want to make is, that during Jesus' ministry they did not believe aright nor did they understand. Regardless of what later Christians may accept or believe, all the evidence suggests that even Jesus' closest associates apparently did not grasp the true meaning of the messianic prophecies or the real meaning of the sacrificial system. In the light of this New Testament evidence, it is likely that even John the Baptist did not really understand what he was saying when he said of Jesus: 'Behold, the lamb of God, who takes away the sin of the world!' (John 1:29, 36). Later, John himself, languishing in prison and deeply torn by doubt, gives utterance to his uncertainty in a pathetic appeal to Jesus: 'Are you he who is to come or shall we look for another?' (Matt. 11:3).

This agonizing question put by John is one which every Christian should seek to answer for himself, and not simply in a superficial way. Should Jesus' messianic claims, rejected by the Jews and so thoroughly misunderstood during the years of Jesus' earthly ministry, be so glibly and light-heartedly accepted by those of us who come many years later in the Christian tradition? Should we not also participate in the searching agony of our forefathers as we attempt to make that Christian message our very own?

Speaking now from my own experience, I can say that a little agonizing over Jesus' messianic claims can result in a real blessing, to say nothing of solving a number of problems of interpretation along the way. But I must share with you the route of my pilgrimage so that you can better understand why this best story turns out the way it does.

'MESSIANIC' PROPHECIES

As a young Christian in a conservative Christian environment I was exposed to a fair amount of traditional Christian material. I suspect that anyone who has been an active participant in a conservative Christian community is well aware of the manner in which messianic prophecies have been handled. I will not cite any specific sources, but will simply summarize the general impression that had become part of my own outlook. First, I learned of the hundreds of amazing prophecies which pointed forward to the true Messiah, Jesus of Nazareth. The chances of anyone other than Jesus of Nazareth fulfilling these prophecies was said to be one in millions. Second, the Jewish people had every opportunity to accept Jesus. Not only were the prophecies explicit, leaving them without excuse, but also the sacrificial system pointed them directly to their promised Saviour. Still, they rejected him.

The residual effect of that two-fold emphasis led imperceptibly to the conclusion that the first century Jews were simply stubborn and the disciples were at least blind, if not stupid. But the other side of the coin is even more dangerous from a spiritual point of view, for my suspicions about the Jews and disciples implied that 'we Christians' were not stubborn like they were, and since we clearly understood the prophecies, we were certainly much brighter than the disciples. Now please pardon this rather too-vivid picture. I have probably over-stated the case, but I do think that something like the above scenario does lurk rather ominously in the background of those of us who have grown up with traditional Christianity.

When I first began to look seriously at these Christian claims, I had considerable difficulty in suppressing my uneasiness, for as I began looking at some of the New Testament 'prophecies' I found them less than convincing. The thought crossed my mind more than once: 'If this is what the Christian claim is based on, Christianity is in deep trouble.' Some of the 'proofs' cited in support of Jesus' claims seemed to be so very convincing to the New Testament writers, yet, quite frankly, they made very little sense to me. How could that be? Was Christianity built on a foundation of wood, hay, and stubble, after all? As I recall, I was enjoying a good Christian experience at the time, so there was no immediate danger of my world falling apart, yet I found it very uncomfortable to think that this good experience might possibly be built on sinking sand instead of on solid rock. I thought of the hundreds of years of Christian tradition and of the many noble and helpful Christians that I had known personally. But I also thought of those who had rejected the Christian tradition in favour of a sceptical or even atheistic position. All these thoughts went tumbling through my head.

But before we look at the solution which I have since found so helpful, let me give you a more specific glimpse of the kinds of difficulties that began to gnaw at my certainties. For sake of convenience, we may note several 'prophecies' from the Gospel of John, all of which are cited from Psalm 69.

1. 'Zeal for thy house will consume me' (John 2:17). This statement is one that the disciples 'remembered' after they had watched Jesus' cleansing the temple. The original reference is found in Ps. 69:9.

2. 'They hated me without a cause' (John 15:25). Jesus applied this statement from Ps. 69:4 to himself as he described the hatred which the world has against him and his Father. The quotation from the psalm is prefaced with the following words: 'It is to fulfil the word that is written in their law.' The relationship of this word 'fulfil' to our word 'prophecy' is one that we will discuss later in the chapter; it can be the source of considerable difficulty.

3. Jesus is given vinegar 'to fulfil the scripture' (John 19:28). This comment by the gospel writer that the vinegar offered to Jesus was to 'fulfil' scripture, seems to be a direct reference to Psalm 69:21. In contrast to the previous two examples, the Old Testament passage is not actually quoted, yet the inference is clear enough.

Now if you want to experience the same kind of difficulty that I did, go directly to Psalm 69, read it through in its entirety, noting how each of these quotations or allusions is used in the original psalm. Incidentally, you may have noted that the three quotations I have cited are of three slightly different types: the first is attributed to the disciples, the second directly to Jesus, while the third is a comment supplied by the gospel writer himself. Similar examples could be noted almost at random throughout the New Testament, though it is in the gospels and Acts that there is most interest in the 'fulfilment' of prophecy.

Looking specifically at Psalm 69, we must ask what the likely conclusion of the Old Testament reader would have been if he were hearing or reading this psalm in the Old Testament context. Would he have seen this psalm and these phrases as 'prophecies' of Jesus' mission? Frankly, I do not see how he could possibly have done so. The psalm is simply a lament by an individual, who is not named in the psalm, although the title does identify it as a 'Psalm of David'. That phrase could easily imply Davidic author-ship (the traditional interpretation), but the original Hebrew could just as easily mean a psalm 'to' David, 'for' David, 'about' David, or 'in honour of' David. Many scholars who would not hold to Davidic authorship in the strict sense do think that the speaker was at least one of Israel's kings in the Davidic line.)

For the purposes of our discussion, let us assume that this is a psalm written by David himself. Would the Old Testament reader have seen the true Messiah in this psalm? The New Testament writers obviously did, and we shall return to that in a moment. But for the Old Testament reader, the matter would not have been at all clear. In the first instance, the psalm is written by someone who considered himself to be a sinner: 'O God, thou knowest my folly; the wrongs I have done are not hidden from thee' (Ps. 69:5). The New Testament claim for Jesus is that he was without sin (cf. Heb. 4:15), so on that point alone we have a definite cleavage between the Old Testament passage and the New Testament fulfilment; at least that is what it appears to be at first glance.

What is even more striking as we compare the content of this psalm with Jesus' experience, is the remarkable contrast in attitudes towards one's enemies. Certainly the Christian would accept the attitude of Jesus on the cross as *the* Christian ideal: 'Father, forgive them; for they know not what they do' (Luke 23:34). But if you want to singe your polite Christian ears, read Psalm 69:22–28. Such venomous words are hard to imagine on the lips of our Lord. We shall approach the problem of violent language more directly in our next chapter. But for our purposes here, it is sufficient to note that there is a great gulf between the experience described in the psalm and that of our Lord. When the psalmist was given vinegar to drink (Ps. 69:21), he erupted into violent curses; when Jesus was given vinegar to drink, he prayed for his tormentors.

So there is the problem: the Old Testament psalm was

written by a sinner who was still struggling with vengeful feelings towards his enemies. Furthermore, the psalm itself gives no clue that it was pointing forward to a future Messiah. Is this the kind of foundation on which Jesus' messianic claim was based? It was at this point that I began a serious search to see if perhaps there might be other prophecies which were more worthy of the name. Of course, there is also the matter of the integrity of Jesus and the New Testament writers. When Jesus himself makes statements that I have difficulty in accepting, that is indeed a question I must face if I take my Christian experience seriously.

Rather than let the solution to the above problems emerge gradually in the course of the chapter, I think it would be helpful to outline briefly my suggested solution. Then we can look at the various parts in greater detail. In short, I believe God's people have appealed to different reasons at different times to establish the same belief in the Messiah. Thus the 'prophecies' of the Messiah can be divided into four basic categories:

1. Those prophecies that were evident to the reader of the Old Testament as pointing toward to one who was to come. These could be recognized as messianic prophecies by any honest reader.
2. Those prophecies which Jesus applied to himself and his mission as a result of his own self-understanding and from his own study of Scripture. According to the evidence we have, application of these prophecies to the Messiah in the way that Jesus understood them was something fresh and original or, at least, his emphasis was different from that of known Jewish teachings about the Messiah.
3. 'Prophecies' which were discovered and applied as the events themselves took place or shortly thereafter, a type of 'prophecy' which was exceptionally popular in the New Testament era and is frequently found in the New Testament itself.
4. 'Prophecies' that were applied to Jesus' mission in later Christian centuries.

Before we look at each of these categories, it would be well to remind ourselves that, in the course of human experience, finding new reasons for old beliefs and practices is nothing unusual. To cite a rather mundane example, note all the various reasons one could give in support of vegetarianism: ascetic (meat tastes good, therefore should be avoided); health (a vegetable diet leads to better health); humanitarian (be kind to animals); ecological (it is wasteful to feed grain to animals and then eat the animals); religious (animals are sacred so should not be killed, much less eaten). It is unlikely that anyone would hold all those arguments at the same time, or with equal intensity. Furthermore, quite different emphases will be found at different eras in history and in different parts of the world. Applying this observation to the interpretation of Scripture, a similar process can be seen at work as God's people find new reasons for supporting old beliefs. I think there is no place where that is more evident than in the promises and prophecies of the Messiah. This point will become clearer as we look at examples for each of the four categories.

1. Messianic Prophecies understandable to the Old Testament believer

This category is the most basic one, for without a substantial foundation at this level, no one would have expected a Messiah at all. With our twentieth century orientation, we are inclined to think that if a prophecy is really a prophecy, it should be seen as such *in advance* of the event or person it foretells. That is so obvious to us that even to make the point seems unnecessary. Yet that is precisely the cause of the difficulty, for the New Testament uses the language of prophecy, foretelling, and foreseeing with reference to persons and events that can really be recognized only by hindsight. We shall return to that point below, but here we must look at some of those prophecies which, in Old Testament times, had the potential to kindle the messianic fires in the hearts of God's people.

Just a comment first, however, on the more technical usage of the terms 'Messiah' and 'messianic'. In our discussion in the last chapter, we noted that the Hebrew word *mashiah* simply means 'anointed one'. In the course of time, however, Israel applied it more specifically to the king as *the* anointed one. Finally, the people began to look to the future and the *ideal* anointed one. So, technically speaking, 'messianic' refers to those prophecies which pointed to a coming royal figure, a descendant in the Davidic line. In traditional Christian interpretation, however, the word has taken on a much broader meaning so that almost anything in the Old Testament can fall under the heading 'messianic' if it points forward in any way to the coming Redeemer. In this connection, it is interesting to note that the Norwegian scholar, Sigmund Mowinckel chose a neutral title for his basic scholarly study of the 'messianic' prophecies of the Old Testament: *He That Cometh*. Thus he could legitimately discuss not just the 'messianic' prophecies, but the full spectrum of Old Testament types which point forward to Christ: king, prophet, servant, and son of man. His title is simply the echo of John the Baptist's searching question: 'Are you the one who is to come, or are we to look for another? (Matt. 11:3). The more technical meaning for 'Messiah' and 'messianic' will explain why I have sometimes used quotation marks to set off these terms: I am simply attempting to get the best of both worlds, the traditional and the technical.

Turning now to specific prophecies, we look first to the initial section of the Hebrew canon: the law of Moses, the Pentateuch. Here, Genesis 49:10 and Numbers 24:17 stand out as the most important verses that point forward to one who is to come. Both are rather cryptic and their broader implications are not at all clear to us, but Jewish interpreters clearly accepted these as 'messianic' even though they did not accept Jesus as the Messiah.

In *Genesis 49:10*, the classic King James Version of Jacob's blessing on his son Judah is quite familiar to Christian ears: 'The sceptre shall not depart from Judah, nor a lawgiver from between his feet, until Shiloh come; and unto him shall the gathering of the people be.' From Judah, someone was to come who would be the focal point of the people's hope. The passage says very little more than that, but it is enough.

Numbers 24:17 is part of Balaam's prophecy about Israel. Again in KJV phraseology: 'I shall see him, but not now: I shall behold him, but not nigh: there shall come a Star out of Jacob, and a Sceptre shall rise out of Israel, and shall smite the corners of Moab, and destroy all the children of Sheth.' Here was someone who would one day smash Israel's enemies. Although the term 'Messiah' does not appear, this passage was 'messianic' for the Jews, and is part of the reason why the Jews and Jesus' own disciples were looking for a heavy-handed Messiah who would smash the enemies of the nation.

In connection with the evidence from the Pentateuch, we should touch on the question of the sacrificial system. Was not this a clear picture of the person and work of the Messiah? A picture, yes, but apparently not a clear one. Where in the Old Testament can you find an *explicit* interpretation of the sacrificial system as applying to the person of the Messiah? Nowhere. Our interpretations of the sacrificial system are from the New Testament. The book of Hebrews is, of course, a powerful exposition of the meaning of the sacrificial system in terms of the mission of Jesus the Messiah. But significantly, Hebrews comes after the death of Jesus, not before. Likewise, the imagery of Jesus as our high priest is primarily the result of inspired reflection on the completed work of Jesus in the light of the sacrificial system. The idea of a royal priest is suggested by Psalm 110:4, but the development of that idea takes place after the cross.

As I have reflected on the way that conservative Christians have dealt with the sacrificial system, I have concluded that we have perhaps confused the type and the anti-type, the shadow and the reality (cf. Heb. 10:1). I mean that we have treated the Old Testament sacrificial system almost as though it were clearer than the real event in Jesus Christ. No wonder that we are quite mystified by the Jewish rejection and the dullness of the disciples. If we assume that the sacrificial system was crystal clear, then it loses its value as shadow and becomes the real thing. That is most unfortunate, for the blood of goats and bulls can never be as meaningful as the death of our Lord on the cross.

As for my own view, I do believe the Old Testament

believer could gain many of the essential principles of God's plan of salvation from a study of the sacrificial system. Some of the great men of God may even have caught glimpses in the sacrifices of the death of the one who was to come. Yet interestingly enough, not even one of the Old Testament writers has seen fit to pass along those insights to us; our book of Hebrews is in the New Testament, not in the Old.

I think you will already begin to see the significance of this conclusion for the interpretation of the experience of the disciples and the Jews: they had not yet linked the 'royal' prophecies with the 'suffering' ones. That was something that God in the flesh must do in their presence. Even then it was very difficult to give up old cherished ideas. But is that not precisely the great danger that faces us every day? We all too easily fall into merely traditional ways of thinking and fail to agonize for the fresh and invigorating vision of truth which comes from a total commitment to our God.

The Pentateuch contains one more 'messianic' prophecy that we should note, namely, the promise in *Deuteronomy 18:15–19* of a great prophet like Moses who would come some day in the future. The promise was given by Moses to the people as he prepared them for his own departure. The passage does not say when or how such a prophet would come. The Lord had simply promised the people that the prophet would be like Moses and would come from among their brethren (Deut. 18:18).

It is instructive to note how the New Testament deals with this promise of the prophet. According to the record in the Gospel of John, the people did not necessarily identify 'the prophet' with the 'Christ' (Messiah), for they asked John the Baptist first if he were 'the Christ,' then if he were 'Elijah' and then if he were 'the prophet' (John 1:21, 25). In other words, they had three distinct figures in mind. Yet John's Gospel also suggests that when Jesus had fed the five thousand, the people were ready to accept him as 'the prophet' while also being ready to proclaim him king (John 6:13–14). After the death of Christ, there is also at least a hint in Stephen's speech that this prophecy of a prophet was applied to Jesus, though the identification is not explicit (Acts 7:37). But in any event, the promise of a prophet was clearly part of the fuel that kindled the people's hopes for the future.

Turning to the prophetic books, we now find messianic prophecies in the precise sense of the word. The prophets were writing in the days of the kings, at a time when the people as well as the prophets had begun to realize that none of their kings had lived up to God's great ideal. Through the prophets, God began to direct the hopes of the people to that ideal future king from the house of David. Here, then, are the true promises of the Messiah, the anointed one who would redeem his people. Let us note a sample of some of the more notable passages.

Isaiah 9:2–7 This prophecy speaks clearly of the throne of David (vs. 7), thus indicating its proper messianic character. But from the standpoint of the New Testament and its claims for Jesus, the most fascinating part of this prophecy is the list of titles given in verse 6: 'For to us a child is born . . . Wonderful Counsellor, Mighty God, Everlasting Father, Prince of Peace.' The Jewish leaders of Jesus' day had great difficulty in accepting Jesus' claims to divinity. They were thinking of a great leader in the Davidic succession, but tended to regard him as a *human* figure who would introduce the Kingdom of Yahweh. When Jesus claimed to be *both* this human *Messiah* and *God*, they were startled. Yet here in Isaiah is a key reference suggesting that the child who was to come would indeed be the mighty God.

Isaiah 11:1–9 This prophecy describes how the 'shoot from the stump of Jesse' would introduce the great and peaceful kingdom of the future. The Spirit of God would be upon him (vs. 2) and he would judge the poor in righteousness (vs. 4). The climax? The earth would be full of the knowledge of Yahweh as the waters cover the sea (vs. 9). With a prophecy like that, who wouldn't long for the coming of the Messiah?

Jeremiah 23:5–6 Jeremiah lived through the tragic demise of the southern kingdom of Judah and saw the last kings of Judah killed or deported to Babylon. He had every reason to be disheartened. Nevertheless, this man of God pointed to a great future king from the line of David;

Yahweh will raise up for David a righteous Branch (vs. 5) and this is the name by which he will be called, 'Yahweh is our righteousness'. The idea of a human king taking the name of Yahweh to himself must have been a troublesome thought for traditional Jews. Yet this passage is part of the evidence which lay behind Jesus' claim that he and his Father were one (John 10:30). Or to paraphrase another famous saying: 'If you have seen me, you have seen Yahweh' (John 14:9).

The emphasis on the royal figure who was to come, the proper messianic figure, may at least partially explain why the royal psalms (i.e. psalms which speak of the king) were such fertile ground for other 'messianic' prophecies. The psalms repeatedly speak of the king as the anointed one, and often bring the anointed one into very close relationship with Yahweh himself (cf. Ps. 2:7). Psalm 110, a very popular New Testament 'messianic' psalm, though apparently not one that was so viewed by the Jews, also makes that famous declaration: 'You are a priest for ever after the order of Melchizedek' (Ps. 110:4). The Old Testament itself does not develop this idea of a priest-king, but the suggestion is there and was destined to be developed in great detail in the light of the cross of Christ.

From the third section of the Hebrew Bible, the Writings, one other passage should be mentioned in connection with the Old Testament 'messianic' evidence, namely, *Daniel 7:13*. Here, the other-worldly figure of the 'son of man' appears. 'Son of man' was a title that the New Testament writers often used for Jesus. In fact, it was one of Jesus' favourite titles for himself. The precise meaning of 'son of man' in the New Testament has been much discussed and we shall not even touch on that discussion here, but we should note that the 'son of man' in Daniel 7:13 is a celestial being who comes from heaven. Hence the imagery of Daniel 7 helps to prepare the way for the claims of Jesus that he was indeed of heavenly origin.

Now after this brief survey of Old Testament evidence, it should be clear enough that the messianic hope at the time of Christ rested on a solid basis. Indeed, the evidence from the New Testament itself testifies that everyone was looking for the Messiah. So in the first century AD, the question most certainly was not *whether* a Messiah was coming or not. That was a foregone conclusion; the Messiah *was* coming. Rather, it was quite a different question that Jesus brought to the attention of his listeners: 'What kind of Messiah are you expecting?' The Gospel of John describes how the people were ready to take Jesus and make him king after he had fed the five thousand (John 6:14–15). But when Jesus revealed the spiritual nature of his kingdom, they turned away in droves (John 6:66).

A superficial reading of the 'messianic' prophecies could indeed suggest the popular conception that the Messiah was to be a conquering king who would smash Israel's enemies. But such a conclusion could come only from a superficial reading of Scripture. When we make a total commitment to righteousness, to truth, to God, the Scriptures come alive with a mysterious glory which quite eludes the casual reader. And that is precisely what happened in Jesus' experience. As he grew in his knowledge of God, the radical nature of his mission was dawning ever more clearly upon him. At the age of twelve the depth of his understanding was already a cause of amazement to the learned rabbis (Luke 2:47). But the time was not yet right; Jesus returned to his home and was subject to his parents (Luke 2:51).

In that home in Nazareth many things must have happened which helped prepare Jesus for his mission. The biblical record is mysteriously silent about these years in Nazareth, but knowing what we do about men of spiritual power, we can be sure that Jesus was deeply immersed in a growing relationship with his heavenly father. The quality of his prayer life and the depth of his study must have been incredible, for when he finally stepped to the threshold of the world to announce his mission to the universe, the crowds 'were astonished at his teaching, for he taught them as one who had authority' (Matt. 7:29). What gave his words that ring of authority? His relationship to his Father, to be sure, but our question must now be not just *how* he taught, but *what* he taught, and that is the matter to which we now turn, for Jesus brought fresh insight and a new emphasis to the messianic prophecies which the disciples simply could not accept, even though they did believe Jesus was the Messiah. It is this unbelievable aspect of Jesus' ministry that we find developed in the second category of 'messianic' prophecies, namely, those that Jesus himself brought to the attention of the people.

2. *Messianic prophecies which became clear as a result of the teaching of Jesus*

The outstanding example in this category of 'messianic' prophecies is none other than Isaiah 53, the prophecy of the suffering servant. For those of us who have been steeped in the New Testament understanding of Jesus' life and message, one of the most obvious and significant aspects of his experience is his suffering and death. Yet before his death this was just the point that virtually everyone around Jesus refused to accept, including those who accepted him as the promised redeemer.

In my own study of the 'messianic' prophecies, it came as a real shock to realize that it was Jesus himself who brought the ministry of the suffering servant into focus as one of the 'messianic' prophecies. Yet after the shock had worn away, I began to realize that this was the only logical conclusion that I could draw from the New Testament evidence. The Jews were inclined to reject Jesus completely; the disciples and the crowds (at least for a while) wanted to make him king; but no one wanted to accept him as the suffering servant.

Jesus must have realized the immense challenge that faced him in the form of the popular concept of the Messiah. To help the people realize that the Messiah must first suffer before he could rule was no easy task. In this connection it is fascinating to note how Jesus dealt with some of the biblical data touching on his mission. In particular, his treatment of Isaiah 61 during the synagogue service of Nazareth is remarkable. As he read the familiar words of the prophet, the anticipation of the people must have been building towards the expected climax: 'The Spirit of the Lord is upon me, because he has anointed me to preach good news to the poor. He has sent me to proclaim release to the captives and recovering of sight to the blind, to set at liberty those who are oppressed, to proclaim the acceptable year of the Lord' (Luke 4:18–19). But then came a real surprise, for the assembled congregation must have been waiting for the next line: 'The day of vengeance of our God' (Is. 61:2). That was what they all longed to see and hear. Instead, Jesus sat down, saying: 'Today this scripture has been fulfilled in your hearing' (Luke 4:21). The congregation's reaction was at first favourable to his 'gracious words' (cf. vs. 21), but then the true implications began to emerge and this Sabbath congregation turned into a ferocious mob, intent on murder (vs. 29). Going against established tradition is hard work, and dangerous. But Jesus knew all about that and he carried on.

Before we move beyond Jesus' mission and his own self-understanding, a further word about Isaiah 53 might be helpful. In the first instance, the passage itself nowhere links the servant with the royal 'Messiah.' The servant is obviously close to Yahweh, but he is not identified as a royal figure. For this reason, scholars have debated endlessly as to the original intent of the prophecy. Again, we cannot go into detail here; for our purposes, it is simply important to know that Jesus himself was apparently the first to link publicly this famous passage with the role of the Messiah. But in this connection something remarkable emerges from Jewish sources, for there is clear evidence that the Jewish community did, in fact, interpret Isaiah 53 messianically, but their messianic interpretation bears almost no relationship to the biblical passage. In fact, they have taken this marvellous passage telling of the servant's lamb-like willingness to suffer on behalf of his people, and have turned it completely on its head, rephrasing it so that it becomes a hymn praising a warrior Messiah who makes the other nations suffer. That was just the messianic view which was prominent in Jesus' day. When the community of God's people could take the very passage which should have opened their eyes to a spiritual kingdom, transforming it to serve their own preconceived ideas, we can appreciate the tremendous challenge facing Jesus as he sought to break through to their hearts and share the good news of a Messiah who gently cares for the suffering sinner. The people wanted no part in such a Messiah, so they destroyed him as a threat to their established tradition. But in so doing, they unwittingly brought to fulfilment those very prophecies which Jesus had brought to light and which have become so central to the Christian understanding of the Messiah.

The fuller meaning of Jesus' self-sacrifice began to emerge among Jesus' followers after the resurrection. As the Christian community reflected on Jesus' earthly experience, they began to see the Old Testament in a radically new light. They began to interpret the Old Testament with renewed enthusiasm. That is why our study of the post-resurrection development of the messianic theme is so crucial. For us the word 'prophecy' always implies foresight, but the kinds of messianic prophecies I have included in the third category seem to involve a generous portion of hindsight. It is to these 'prophecies' that we now turn.

3. *Prophecies discovered and applied in light of the events themselves*

This category of messianic prophecies is undoubtedly the most prominent and most popular with the New Testament writers, but it is probably the most difficult one for the modern reader to comprehend. In my own study of messianic prophecies I struggled to make sense out of this type of 'prophecy' and to maintain the integrity of the New Testament writers. In the course of my education, even in connection with the Bible, perhaps especially in connection with the Bible, it had been deeply drilled into my head that I must read according to the author's intent. I learned that I must never cite an author as proving the point that I am attempting to make if he himself obviously has something quite different in mind. My problem threatened to become acute when I tried to apply this rule to the New Testament writers and discovered that when they cited the Old Testament authors, they often departed far from the obvious meaning of the Old Testament passage. So I was faced with two alternatives, equally unattractive. First, I could force myself to believe that the Old Testament authors actually said what the New Testament writers claimed for them. In other words, the New Testament writers were always right and their interpretation would take precedence over what I thought the Old Testament writers originally meant. The other alternative seemed to be to admit that the New Testament writers were wrong in citing the Old Testament in the way they did. In such a case I seemed to be admitting that the New Testament writers were unreliable, and therefore the point that they were arguing, namely, that Jesus was the promised Messiah, was open to question.

As I have suggested earlier, it was at this point that I began to look for more substantial prophecies. The more important of these I have already noted in category one. That, at least, helped to buy a little time as I continued to struggle with the New Testament authors. I was so long in solving the problem for myself and yet the solution now seems so very simple, that I am sometimes perplexed as to how I can best share the good news. But the news is so good that I must at least attempt to share it.

The solution to this third category lies in two parts. First, in an understanding of how God has worked through his inspired writers, and second, in an understanding of some of the popular forms of argument employed by Jewish writers in and around the first century AD. Both of these aspects merit further discussion.

In the first instance, I discovered that I had fallen victim to a way of thinking about God and his word that had contributed to my difficulty. My thinking went something like this: God is perfect, the Bible is God's words, therefore the Bible is perfect. Now I would hasten to add that the Bible is perfect for the purpose for which God intended it, but that is a far cry from being perfect in the same sense that God is perfect. God's word must be compared with the incarnation: the perfection of divinity is clothed with the imperfection and weakness of human flesh. I had tended to think that the logic and rhetoric of the human writers was in fact God's logic and rhetoric. It is not. Scripture reflects the logic and rhetoric of human beings who are speaking God's message under the guidance of his Spirit, but they are also very much under the influence of their own limitations of language, character, knowledge and ability. The Spirit controls the process to the extent that from the writings of these inspired men the sincere seeker for truth can indeed learn what he needs to know about God, but the bits and pieces, especially when taken in isolation and apart from God's intention to communicate the truth, can be very misleading. If an inspired writer is a highly educated individual and has a good grasp of language, he will write accordingly. If, by contrast, a writer comes from an unsophisticated background, he will reveal this background by his homely language, his earthy illustrations and his rough logic. The Spirit does not obliterate these human elements.

How does this apply to our understanding of 'messianic' prophecies? In just this way, that the New Testament writers were men of the first century, and since God chose to reveal his will in the first century, he inspired men to give his message in the accepted thought forms of the first century. Here is where the second part of the solution comes in, for when I began to realize the kind of thinking and the kind of logic that was prominent in Jewish sources of the early Christian era, I began to recognize something terribly familiar, namely, precisely those problem arguments that I had found in the New Testament. In short, the New Testament writers were using standard and accepted Jewish methods of treating Scripture when they seemingly departed into such flights of fancy. Remarkably, there is no evidence in the New Testament that the Jewish opponents of the Christian community argued against their methodology; they were quite accustomed to that. They argued, rather, with the Christian conclusion. They were not prepared to accept the suffering servant as their Messiah, even if the Christians used all the right methods in proving their point. But we need to illustrate this conclusion from the New Testament and from Jewish sources, something that I think we can do fairly quickly and briefly.

The one feature of Jewish methodology that is particularly pertinent for us is the tendency to read later events back into earlier narratives. Without the knowledge of these later events, no one would have dreamed of them on the basis of the earlier narratives. But once the events became known, Jewish rabbis loved to 'discover' them in the earlier passages. In the rabbinic discussions, then, it became customary for the rabbis to debate among themselves just which events were 'foretold' in which narratives. To illustrate this way of treating Scripture, we could turn almost at random to any of the ancient Jewish commentaries on Scripture, a type of commentary known as Midrash. Many of these commentaries are available in English translation and provide a fascinating insight into Jewish methods of interpreting Scripture.

For our purposes, a glimpse at the Midrash on Genesis 15:17–18[1] should serve quite well. In interpreting the phrase: 'Behold a smoking furnace and a flaming torch, Simeon Ben Abba said in the name of a yet more famous rabbi, Rabbi Johanan, that in this vision God had revealed four things to Abraham: Gehenna (hell), the kingdoms that would oppress Israel (Egypt, Babylon, Persia, Media, Rome), Revelation, and the Temple. The Midrash then records the rabbinical discussions about the fuller implication of the suggested interpretation. Now if we look at the original Genesis context, none of these four things is at all explicit. The verses immediately preceding (Gen. 15:13–16) do speak of subjugation to a nation which turned out to be Egypt. But in the light of later Jewish history and theology, the rabbis went far beyond the biblical narrative, expanding on the 'smoking furnace' to include the negative elements of hell and oppression, while interpreting a 'flaming torch' as referring to the positive aspects of Revelation and the Temple. All of this was by way of hindsight, yet the rabbis commented on the passage in such a way as to suggest that Abraham could see this complete picture.

From this same section of the Midrash, a fascinating variation on this Jewish methodology can be illustrated,

1 See Midrash Rabbah on Genesis, XLIV, 21–22 (English translation published by the Soncino Press, London)

namely, the use of an individual word occurring in one passage to expand the content of another verse where the same word appears. For example, Rabbi Joshua claimed that this experience of Abraham indicates that God had revealed the dividing of the Red Sea to Abraham. How did he arrive at that remarkable interpretation? The key lies in the Hebrew word for 'pieces' (*gezarim*) which appears in the phrase: 'and a flaming torch passed between these *pieces*' (Gen. 15:17). This is the same Hebrew word which appears in Ps. 136:13. The KJV translates it as 'parts' (*gezarim*) in the phrase: (O give thanks) . . . 'to him which divided the Red Sea into *parts*.' Rabbi Joshua assumed that the content of the verse in Psalm 136 (dividing of the Red Sea) must have been included in the earlier experience of Abraham since the biblical narrative uses the same word (*gezarim*) in both passages. He concluded, therefore, that God had revealed the dividing of the Red Sea to Abraham. Remarkable!

These examples are quite typical of rabbinical interpretation of Scripture. And since the New Testament writers were thoroughly immersed in this first-century Jewish culture, they could without hesitation, use these methods. Whenever I read through early Jewish sources, I think I detect a certain excitement as the rabbis make fresh 'discoveries' in what, to us, almost seems like a sacred game with words. But they were quite serious. So were the New Testament writers.

Given this Jewish background, I can now appreciate the way in which some early Christians excitedly mined the Old Testament for fresh 'prophecies' of this Messiah whom they had already accepted on quite other grounds. These 'prophecies' were not the foundation of Jesus' messianic mission; they were simply later confirmations of something his followers already believed. To be sure, the apostles used these methods in their evangelism, for they were working largely with Jews. Now if we can understand this early Judeo-Christian environment, we no longer need to fault the integrity of the New Testament writers, nor will we fault God for using men who employed such strange methods. God has always used men within their own environment to speak to their contemporaries. It is our responsibility to understand them so that we can understand God's message to them and through them, a message which he has intended for us also.

When we recognize that the 'messianic' prophecies of categories 1 and 2 formed the basis for the disciples' convictions, then perhaps we can more readily grant them the privilege of using the category 3 prophecies, prophecies which carried a fair bit of weight in their own day, but which seem so strange from the standpoint of our way of reasoning. But let us look now at how the New Testament actually uses this Jewish methodology to establish the messianic claims of Jesus.

Peter's speech on the day of Pentecost provides us with a good example of the apostolic method of dealing with the Old Testament messianic 'prophecies'. In Acts 2:23 Peter refers to 'the definite plan and foreknowledge of God' that the Jews would deliver up Jesus to be crucified. Then he refers to a Davidic psalm, Psalm 16, saying that David was speaking 'of him', that is, of Jesus (Acts 2:25). Turning back to Psalm 16, I find nothing at all that would indicate to the Old Testament reader that this psalm was pointing forward to the Messiah. It appears simply to be a psalm of thanksgiving for the fact that God has preserved his own. True, the psalm is royal and Davidic, thus linking it loosely with the messianic tradition, but for us to accept that the psalmist wanted his readers to think of *the* Messiah is hardly a conclusion that we can draw on the basis of the Old Testament. Yet Peter makes the statement: 'David says concerning him' and by 'him', Peter is clearly referring to Jesus the Messiah. Now judged by our way of thinking we might be inclined to say that Peter was wrong. But such a conclusion does not take into account the accepted methods of Peter's day. Peter was not wrong; he was simply making use of the Jewish methodology described above which allows the inclusion of later events in earlier passages. Peter can actually go on to say that David was a prophet (Acts 2:30), and that he 'foresaw' and 'spoke of the resurrection of the Christ, and that he was not abandoned to Hades, nor did his flesh see corruption' (Acts 2:31). He uses all the language of prophecy. And that can cause us great difficulty if we do not realize how earlier passages can be made to 'prophesy' in the light of later events simply by the use of good Jewish methodology. In other words, it is essential that we recognize how the word 'prophecy' could be very much expanded in the first century AD so that it could refer, not just to foresight, but to hindsight as well. Such an understanding of 'prophecy' provides the clue for understanding the great number of messianic citations in the New Testament which simply do not seem to be predictions in their original Old Testament setting. And I would include here the citations out of Psalm 69 in the Gospel of John which we noted earlier. The original passages were not predictions, but the first century methodology made it possible to turn them into such. The New Testament writers 'found' many of these 'prophecies' and did not hesitate to use them, for the New Testament is full of them.

In this connection it would be well to note how conservative Christians have often reacted against the conclusions of modern scholars who initially may have had nothing more sinister in mind than simply to call attention to the fact that the Old Testament passages do not say to us what the New Testament writers understood them to say to them. A modern scholar might say: 'Psalm 16:10 does not really predict the resurrection of Christ.' To which the conservative response has often been: 'Yet it must, for the New Testament says it does.' Without an understanding of the Jewish methods behind the New Testament quotations, the choice would appear to be between scholarship and piety: if we accept the scholarly point of view, we must reject the New Testament; to accept the New Testament point of view, we must reject the scholarly position. Such a stark dichotomy can be avoided if we understand, first, how God has worked in Scripture, and second, how first century Jews interpreted the Old Testament.

I should further emphasize that a belief in the resurrection of Christ does not at all depend on the use of a particular Old Testament text. The resurrection stands on the basis of the New Testament narrative just as we noted earlier that the Virgin Birth is established on the basis of Matthew, not Isaiah. To be sure, the New Testament writers constantly bring these additional passages into use, but they must be seen as additional proofs for a Jewish audience, not as primary evidence for the twentieth century reader. We need not sacrifice a single cardinal point of faith; we simply need to be careful that we use the reasons that are most likely to be cogent for our day when we seek to establish those teachings that are important for the Christian faith. As noted earlier, at different times and in different places, different arguments have carried more weight. We must still recognize that these different arguments have been used by men of God, men who were under the guidance of the Holy Spirit. Yet if we are truly guided by the Spirit today, we will not force someone to accept an argument as primary evidence when that argument could be effective only in a quite different culture. When I finally came to understand that point, I made my peace with the writers of the New Testament. They have been good friends of mine ever since.

Before we turn to the fourth and last category of prophecies, we should note how the understanding of a particular word in the New Testament can provide a more specific explanation for a number of passages that have been called 'prophecies' by Christian interpreters. The key word is 'fulfil,' one that is particularly prominent in the gospels. We have already noted the use of this word in several contexts, most notably in connection with the Virgin Birth and Isaiah 7:14//Matt. 1:22–23. But for purposes of illustrating the use of this word, I would like to suggest a comparison between Hosea 11:1 and Matthew 2:15.

The verse in Matthew describes the flight of Jesus and his parents into Egypt. The passage concludes with the following statement: 'This was to fulfil what the Lord had spoken by the prophet, "Out of Egypt have I called my son" ' (Matt. 2:15). At first glance the modern reader might suspect that Matthew is referring to an Old Testament prophecy of the first type, namely, one that clearly predicts the coming of the Messiah to the Old Testament reader. But when we turn to Hosea 11:1, we discover something quite different, for there the passage is clearly referring to the departure of Israel from Egypt at the time of the Exodus. How could that experience predict the coming of Christ to the reader? In the first instance, we must recognize that, at least in part, Matthew is again using typical Jewish methodology in reading later events back into earlier passages. Note, however, that in this instance Matthew does not use the term 'prophecy,' though many later Christian interpreters have not hesitated to do so, contributing to the confusion that we have already discussed. But even though the background of Jewish methodology can be helpful in understanding Matthew's general approach, the really significant clue to understanding this type of 'prophecy' is found in the word 'fulfil'. Behind this word lies a Greek word *pleroō* which means 'to fill full' as well as 'to fulfil.' Selecting the first meaning of the word instead of the second, we could roughly paraphrase what Matthew is saying as follows: 'Those ancient words of the prophet describing how God brought his son out of Egypt have now been filled full of fresh new meaning in the life and ministry of Jesus Christ.' Thus, instead of a prediction which is brought to pass and so 'fulfilled', this way of understanding Matthew sees rather an old story whose words are filled full of fresh new meaning, meaning which, quite literally, had never been thought of before.

This usage of the word 'fulfil' can be illustrated also from Matt. 5:17 where Jesus says that he has not come to destroy the law, but to fulfil it. He then proceeds to show just how he has come to fill the law full of meaning. The law says, for example, 'You shall not kill.' But when we fill the law full of its true meaning we learn that we should not even hate (Matt. 5:21–22). By understanding the word 'fulfil' in this way, we can view many of the Old Testament passages, not as predictions which were fulfilled, but as words that have been filled full of a new and even quite different meaning in the new situation in Jesus Christ.

Briefly summarizing the implications of our discussion of this third category of messianic 'prophecies', we note the following points. First, we must recognize that God works with human beings within their own environment;

his inspired men reflect their human background and training. Having recognized this, we can then move on to the second point, our understanding of the environment of the first century AD. It should be clear from our discussion that rabbinical interpretation of Scripture was often based on methods which seem quite foreign to us. This is particularly noticeable in the tendency to read later events back into earlier narratives. This Jewish background is the explanation for the remarkable 'proofs' sometimes cited by New Testament writers. A third and more specific point, is the usage of the term 'fulfil.' Against the general background of Jewish methodology, the New Testament writers often spoke of later experiences filling old words full of new meaning. Thus 'fulfil' does not really refer to a prediction coming to pass, but to an old narrative coming to life in a new way.

With this look at the New Testament era, we are now prepared to move further afield and note the even later 'discoveries' of additional messianic 'prophecies.'

4. Prophecies understood as messianic in later Christian centuries

In this last category of 'messianic' prophecies we will simply note a couple of 'prophecies' that have been much used through several centuries of Christian interpretation. One such prophecy is the so-called *Protevangelium* (first gospel) of Genesis 3:15: 'I will put enmity between thee and the woman, between thy seed and her seed. It shall bruise thy head, but thou shalt bruise his heel.' This classic KJV rendering is very familiar to Christian ears. In the light of the New Testament imagery of the 'seed' (Christ) and the serpent (Satan), this passage has been taken as intimating the great cosmic struggle between the forces of good and the forces of evil, the conflict between Christ and Satan. The hints are there in the passage, but neither the Old Testament nor the New picked up this passage and applied it to Christ; the application was to come after the close of the canon to Scripture.

One other later discovery of significance is the prophecy

of Daniel 9:24–27. Modern scholarship has tended to deny that Daniel was written in the sixth century, preferring a date close to the time of the Maccabean revolt (c. 165 BC). Such an approach tends to see Daniel not as genuine prophecy, but as history written as prophecy. Conservative Christians, however, have insisted that the book is indeed prophecy, though even so their interpretations have varied considerably. The arguments need not detain us here for our primary purpose is to look at the history of interpretation of Daniel. In this connection, we note that the prophecy of Daniel 9 came to be seen by many Christians as the most important of all messianic prophecies, a prophecy not just of the coming of the Messiah, but of the time of his coming as well. Sir Isaac Newton, for example, in his commentary on Daniel declared that this prophecy was the 'cornerstone' of the Christian faith.

The basis for this interpretation and the considerable variation in dates adopted by different interpreters provide fertile ground for research, but for our purposes it is sufficient to note that the key phrase is found in Daniel 9:27, rendered by the KJV as follows: 'And in the midst of the week he shall cause the sacrifice and the oblation to cease.' When applied to Jesus Christ, this passage is taken to refer to the death of Christ on the cross and the end of the sacrificial system.

Now even though Christians have claimed that this prophecy is a chief 'cornerstone' of the faith, the history of interpretation indicates that it only *gradually* took its place as a cornerstone, for certainly there is little evidence in Scripture or in the early Jewish writings to suggest that this prophecy was used to predict the time or the mission of Jesus. About two hundred years after the birth of Christ, Clement of Alexandria (d. 220) and Tertullian (d. 240), two fathers of the Christian church, did apply the prophecy to the incarnation and death of Christ, but these early interpreters tended to see the prophecy ending at or around AD 70, the time of Jerusalem's destruction by the Romans. The history of the interpretation of Daniel 9:24–27 is a fascinating one, but for our purposes we simply need to emphasize the fact that here is a prophecy which the Christian community 'discovered' many years after

Jesus' earthly ministry. Nevertheless, it has brought a great deal of comfort and encouragement to God's people.

So at the end of our survey, we can affirm that the messianic hope is one that has remained constant through the ages, first in the Old Testament as God's people looked forward with increasing eagerness to the one who was to come. Then, in the person of Jesus Christ, at least some of the Jewish community recognized the One who had come as their Redeemer. Many rejected this gentle man who said that he had come to die for their sins, but many found in him the source of life. These have carried the good news throughout the world, and the word is still being spread abroad today. We may not find equally convincing all the reasons that have been used through the ages to establish the conviction that Jesus of Nazareth was the embodiment of the Old Testament hope. But we should be able to see how God has used many and varied ways to build faith in the hearts of his people.

Recognizing that God has indeed used a great variety of ways in working with man has made it possible for me to build my house of faith on more solid rock. Now when the winds blow, I don't have to be afraid. That has not only been a great relief, but a cause for great joy. Perhaps that is also one of the reasons why I like to think of the hope of the Messiah as the best story in the Old Testament as well as in the New, and indeed anywhere else you might care to look. It is good news that is worth sharing.

CHAPTER EIGHT

What kind of Prayers would you publish if you were God?

'My God, my God, why hast thou forsaken me?'
(Psalm 22:1).

Whenever I come to the prayers of the Old Testament, I have difficulty in restraining my enthusiasm, for they have helped me greatly in solving two problems of Christian experience and theology. In fact, my study of Old Testament prayers has brought together these two, apparently distinct, but equally thorny problems, and has shown how one is actually the solution to the other. Now whenever two miserable and unhappy people can get together in a marriage which is both a joy to experience and a joy to behold, that has to be good news. This chapter tells a story something like that.

Now for the two problems. The first one focuses on the psalms; the violence, the self-righteousness, the God-forsakenness, so boldly proclaimed therein. How could inspired writers be so virulent? Is it right for a man of God to breathe vengeance on his enemies? In short, many psalms seem to reflect an experience far from the Christian ideal. For Christians who claim the Bible as the Word of God, the problem is particularly acute, for we cannot simply dismiss a portion of Scripture if it does not suit our fancy. If we wish to remain within that heritage which claims the Bible as the Word of God, we really have only two choices: either we can avoid the difficult parts, or we can try to come to grips with them. This chapter will attempt the latter approach.

The second problem is more difficult to define, but it has to do with the polite distance that sometimes separates a Christian and God, a distance that makes it difficult to be frank and open with one's Maker. I suspect this problem is particularly acute for conservative Christians who have grown up with a deep appreciation of God's holiness that sometimes borders on fear. There is, of course, a proper fear of the Lord, but there is an improper fear, as well, one that is closer to panic than to respect. In my own experience, this problem did not manifest itself so much as panic, but as an excessive politeness which left my relationship with him ordinary and superficial. Somehow I felt reluctant to tell God where it hurt and when. I was reluctant to confess to him that I did not understand his ways. If my experience was anaemic, I hesitated to admit it. I somehow felt that I had to keep a smile pasted on my face to show him that I was indeed one of his happy children and that all was going well on earth.

Looking back on that experience, I think I have discovered why I tended to be so polite with God: I would cite a couple of horror stories (Uzzah, the bears and the boys, etc.), a few Proverbs (the 'abominations' cf. Prov. 3:32; 12:22; 28:9), a choice morsel from Ecclesiastes ('Be not rash with your mouth . . .' Eccl. 5:2). Such passages, along with a few other oddments from Scripture, all mingled together in the dark recesses of my mind to produce an ominous effect. All these bits and pieces were straight from Scripture, but I don't recall that they were ever being brought forcefully to my attention at any particular point in time. Perhaps I was just a rather sensitive youngster who tended to over-react to rebukes. I don't know. But in any event, my selective memory produced a caricature of God which counteracted my polite public confessions of a God of love. In fact, if you had asked me at any time during my experience about the kind of God I served, I would not have breathed the slightest complaint. I served a good God who loved me and cared for me. But in a sense, I was forced to say those nice things about him, for back there in the dimly lit passages of my mind lay poor

Uzzah and the forty-two boys; right close by stood God with a big stick. So I developed the habit of being quite careful of what I did and said in God's presence. My prayers were polite. Any agony of soul was kept well under cover. After all, who wanted to become an abomination to the Lord?

Now bring the two problems together: the violent and passionate words of the psalms and my polite little prayers to the great God of the universe. You can imagine my initial shock when I actually began to read the psalms. Do you mean to tell me that those were God's men, speaking for God and under the influence of his Spirit? And the Lord did not strike them dead? Such wild prayers and here they were in my Bible! But maybe you haven't read the psalms lately and need a sample to remind you of the kinds of things that at one time threatened to curl my hair. Let me share with you a few of the more lively examples.

Pride of place must go to Psalm 137:9. Here the psalmist breathes out his hatred against one of Israel's long-time enemies, the Edomites, concluding his 'prayer' with the words: 'Happy shall he be who takes your little ones and dashes them against the rock!' Then there is Psalm 17, a good one to lay alongside the New Testament story of the Pharisee and the Publican (Luke 18:9–14): 'Give ear to my prayer from lips free of deceit (v. 1); If thou testest me, thou wilt find no wickedness in me; my mouth does not transgress (v. 3); My steps have held fast to thy paths, my feet have not slipped' (v. 5). Here was a man *truly* thankful that he was not like other men. Finally there is Psalm 22. One of God's men had the gall actually to claim that God had forsaken him (v. 1). Furthermore, this same psalmist bluntly suggested that there was a certain injustice on the part of the Lord, for the Lord had listened to his fathers' prayers, but not to his own (vv. 2–6). Such bravery. Such opening of one's mouth in the presence of God.

I finally awoke to the fact that God's people had been quite frank with him all along. I had simply robbed myself of a great privilege by letting a few stories and a few lines of Scripture loom large and out of proportion to their worth. If David and the psalmists could be open with

God, why couldn't I? And that was the beginning of a real friendship with my God.

THE PROBLEM OF INSPIRATION

But what about the role of the Holy Spirit and 'inspiration' as it relates to these brash prayers? Even though I was willing to admit that certain parts of Scripture were more helpful to me than others, I was not at all willing to concede that there might be degrees of inspiration. And I would still hold most vigorously to a strong position on inspiration. I reject the view that some of the biblical writers were more inspired than others. Either a man is inspired or he is not. As a conservative Christian, I believe that all Scripture is inspired by God (2 Tim. 3:16). That is actually one of the great strengths of the evangelical position, for we cannot be tempted to take out our scissors and snip away that which we cannot understand or cannot accept. Scripture is Scripture and we must continue to grapple with it until we make our peace with it and with God.

How then can we explain those passages of Scripture in which we clearly see a difference in the experience of one writer when compared with another? For example, 'Father, forgive them,' the famous prayer of Jesus for his enemies (Luke 23:34), reflects an experience far superior to that of the psalmist who asks the Lord to smash his opponents (Ps. 69:22–28). We must recognize that difference or we run the risk of wrongfully appealing to the psalmists to support our perverted passions. I think it is safe to conclude that both the mental and the spiritual capabilities of the various writers of Scripture varied greatly and this variation is reflected in their writings. Yet the quality of inspiration is constant throughout. Perhaps a mundane illustration might help. If I take a stack of wet wood and a stack of dry wood and put the same match to both, what will be the result? One will burn bright, clear, and hot. The other will burn reluctantly, with much wheezing and a great deal of smoke. Both are burning, both have been lit by the same match, but the difference in the quality of the raw material makes a great deal of difference in the fire. One can, however, still get warm by both fires, and for some purposes, the smokey, slow burning fire may even be superior. So it is with God's inspired men. The same spirit kindles them all; some will burn more brightly than others, but the Lord can work through them all. We might be inclined to blame the match for the poor fire. Any fault, however, lies not in the match, but in the soggy wood. And surprisingly, in spite of soggy wood, anyone who so desires can be properly warmed even by that smokey fire.

In the college classroom I sometimes draw a comparison between the biblical writers and the productions of the first-year students in college writing. Our particular grading system calls for two marks to be placed on each composition: one for the content and one for the mechanics. Thus a student who is a creative writer but a poor technician can actually receive both an *A* (content) and an *F* (mechanics). With reference to the inspired writers, we could perhaps give one mark for spiritual capability and one for mental. In actual practice, it would be rather difficult to assign marks, except in some of the more notable cases such as we have already mentioned from the psalms. And I would hasten to add that God's messengers never fall below a *C-*, the lowest mark 'with honour' in our system, in spiritual or mental capabilities. In other words, some of the Bible writers may be more brilliant than others, but each is bright enough. Some undoubtedly have a deeper experience than others, but each has an experience deep enough to be used by God.

We should also note that the brilliant student may not always be the best one for the job. Average students who really have had to work for their marks sometimes make the best teachers and the best family doctors. The same holds true of the biblical writers. The varying skills and insights of the various writers can meet the needs of a variety of people. The simple gospel stories may be just what some need, while others prefer to be stimulated by the more complicated logic of the Pauline correspondence. In my case, I needed some really violent prayers from the psalms. So in the end, God's purposes are served very well by the great variety of writers and the differences in their experiences. Through this variety, there is something in Scripture for everyone.

But returning to the 'problem' psalms, what is the truth that God is trying to tell me, assuming that he is not trying to tell me to smash my enemies? Quite frankly, I think the great 'truth' of many of the psalms lies in the openness and the frankness which characterizes the relationship between the psalmist and God. Even though these men still have much growing to do, they have great confidence in God. They trust him. And they can tell him when and where it hurts.

We should note, however, that there are more signs of growth in the psalms than might first meet the eye. For example, the psalmists are generally quite willing to grant God the privilege of taking vengeance on their enemies. That is not a 'natural' human response. Our human tendency is to take justice into our own hands: 'If you even touch me, I'll smash you!' The classic biblical example of this burning thirst for vengeance is found in the experience of Lamech, the descendant of Cain: 'I have slain a man for wounding me, a young man for striking me. If Cain is avenged sevenfold, truly Lamech seventy-sevenfold' (Gen. 4:23–24). That is precisely what happens in all those troubled areas of our world where strife never ceases: a constant battle to strike the last and the heaviest blow, a constant manoeuvring to thrust in the last and most cutting word. That is human nature. But the psalmist was willing to leave it to the Lord, a truly remarkable step in the right direction. He may still be seething, but the Lord will have to be the one to even the score. There are exceptions to this pattern, even in the psalms, but it is truly remarkable how the psalmists seem to feel that if they pour out their feelings to God, all will be well.

PRAYING WITH THE PSALMISTS

So how do I pray, now that I have heard such lively, vivid, and almost disrespectful prayers in the psalms? In the first place, my polite, all-is-well approach has disappeared. I have discovered after considerable reflection, that I had, in effect, fallen into a form of righteousness by works. For when I felt that my feelings were unworthy to lay before the Lord and that my soul was too sordid to appear in his presence, I was essentially telling myself that I had to tidy myself up first before I could come to him. If *only* those with clean hands and a pure heart can ascend the hill of the Lord (Ps. 24:4), then who will help the sinner? I cannot stifle my feelings of vengeance or my pharisaical pride. Only the Lord can cure ills of that sort. In fact, there is a beautiful verse in Acts that has helped me to see the larger picture. After the resurrection when Peter and the apostles were speaking before the Jewish leaders, Peter declared that God had exalted Jesus 'to give repentance to Israel' (Acts 5:31). So repentance is a gift from God! How can I change my heart when I 'enjoy' that delicious feeling of revenge that wells up when I have slipped in that last biting word? It is a bitter joy, to be sure, but in our strangely human way, we do enjoy our bitterness, our hatred, and our envy. All we can do is ask the Lord to give us repentance, to take away the bitter joy in our sinning, to make our hearts new in him.

So now I can open my heart to the Lord even when it is deeply soiled—especially when it is soiled—for he is the only source of my help. My prayers may not be quite so polite now, but I serve him with a vigour and a joy which was unknown before. I can tell it like it is, for I serve a great God who has given me the privilege of complaining to him when I feel he has forsaken me. I cherish that privilege and I know it is mine. He has even published a prayer to prove it.

QUESTIONING GOD

There is another aspect of the Old Testament experience that has greatly enriched my prayer life, and that is the great freedom which God's friends exercise in his presence when they don't understand his justice or if they fear that he might be doing something damaging to his own reputation. Now there are passages in Scripture which encourage caution in our conversations with the

Lord, and these have their place (cf. Mal. 3:13–15; Romans 9:20). There is a scepticism that is damaging and destructive and ought to be avoided at all costs. But there is also a healthy doubt that arises from honest questioning, from a sincere desire to know the truth and to see God's kingdom established. It is this latter brand of questioning that is actually quite easily aroused in God's true friends.

One of the most striking examples of such a 'sceptical' friend of God is Job. In ordinary conversation we speak of the 'patience of Job,' but the only place in the book of Job where the 'patience' appears is in the first two chapters. Beginning with chapter 3, Job opens his mouth and curses the day of his birth (Job 3:1). And that is only the beginning. During the course of his conversations with his friends, Job says some startling things about his friends and some shocking things about God. For example, when speaking of God he exclaims: 'It is all one; therefore I say, he destroys both the blameless and the wicked. When disaster brings sudden death, he mocks at the calamity of the innocent' (Job 9:22–23). In fact, I find it fascinating to note how Job is used and quoted in the Christian community, for often the 'noble' sayings cited from the book of Job actually come from the mouths of Job's friends, and they had to repent in the end (cf. Job 42:7–9). If, however, we were to read in the church many of the things that Job said in his distress, the assembled worshippers would be horrified. But in spite of all Job's shocking utterances, when the dust had settled, God declared that Job was the one who had spoken the truth; the friends had uttered lies (Job 42:7). That in itself is a striking illustration of how the larger framework of one's thoughts and motives is much more important than the specific words and sentences. Taken at the level of individual words and sentences, it was Job who blasphemed and the friends who praised. But in terms of the larger picture, Job's apparent blasphemy was transformed into truth, while the praises of the friends called for repentance and restitution. When the heart belongs to God, such a scepticism can be a powerful weapon in the service of the Lord.

Two other stories, this time from the Pentateuch, are

among my favourites for illustrating the openness that
God's friends have towards him. The first story is
Abraham's conversation with God over the fate of Sodom.
I would highly recommend that you read the whole narrative, but especially Genesis 18:22–33. There we see
Abraham's initial reaction when he learned from Yahweh
that the destruction of Sodom and Gomorrah was immi-
nent. He was horrified: 'Wilt thou indeed destroy the
righteous with the wicked?' (v. 23). 'Far be it from thee to
do such a thing, to slay the righteous with the wicked, so
that the righteous fare as the wicked! Far be that from
thee! Shall not the Judge of all the earth do right?' (v. 25).
Now there was a time when I thought that anyone who
would talk like that to God deserved a slap in the face or
something worse. But no. The Lord kept a straight face
and was actually willing to bargain with Abraham. He did
not strike Abraham dead for questioning him. You see,
Abraham was a friend of God and God's friends can afford
to talk frankly with the Lord of the universe. It is interesting to observe, however, the telltale signs that Abraham's
conscience was gently pricking him throughout this
bargaining session with the Lord (vv. 27, 30, 31, 32). Yet
that respectful side of his conscience did not deter him
from thrusting forward the questions which the sceptical
side of his conscience impelled him to ask. And, of course,
Abraham's primary concern was for the reputation of the
great Judge of all the earth. Abraham was a subject of that
great Judge and he was intent that the reputation of his
Judge remain absolutely untarnished. What bravery! What
loyalty! What friendship!

A similar experience is reflected in Moses' relationship
with God. Exodus 32 describes the conversation between
Moses and Yahweh after Israel's great apostasy at Sinai.
The Lord must have been testing Moses to see if his heart
was in the right place when he said, 'Now therefore let me
alone, that my wrath may burn both against them and I
may consume them; but of you I will make a great nation'
(Ex. 32:10). Any normal human being would have jumped
at the chance to become the founder of a great nation, and
especially if one had gone through the agony that Moses
had experienced with Israel. But Moses was no normal

human. He was another one of God's friends and his reaction was immediate: 'Why Lord? What will the Egyptians say? And remember the promises you made to Abraham, Isaac, and Israel. You even swore to them by yourself. Repent of this evil and turn from your fierce wrath' (see Ex. 32:11–14). 'And the Lord repented of the evil which he thought to do to his people' (Ex. 32:14). When the right people are sceptical with God at the right time, they can even save whole nations. At least that is what happened when Moses opened his heart to the Lord.

SOME BASIC PRINCIPLES

In conclusion, let us summarize some basic principles that can be of help in dealing with the problems noted at the beginning of the chapter, first, the violence and crudities in the psalms, and second, the difficulty of being really open with a holy God. As I have suggested, the two problems belong together, for when we realize that the psalmists could address God with absolute honesty, we can take heart and do likewise. But we must remember that the violent language in the psalms is not a reflection of the ideal experience; it is not a reflection of God himself, but rather of his erring children who were struggling with life and death issues in a twisted world. Under the impulse of his spirit, they cried to him, baring their souls in a way that often makes us uncomfortable, but their faces were towards God and he listened, even to their uncultured language. From that we can take courage, for whether our souls are bitter, angry, or depressed, when we come to him, we know that he will listen. And that, of course, is the answer to the second problem, the problem of our polite, arms-length conversations with God. Surprisingly, now that I know that the Lord will listen to strong, even seemingly disrespectful language, that very knowledge often takes the edge off my rebellion. Simply knowing that he can handle my seething emotions is often just the tonic that I need to restore my soul to health.

This chapter has described something that is very near to the heart of my Christian experience. Yet even as I bring this chapter and this book to a close, I am aware of the great paradox in the divine-human relationship. As I now reflect on the grandeur and the nearness of my God, his holiness and his friendliness, I feel myself torn between two conflicting emotions. I am drawn by the force of his love, but am forced to my knees by the awareness of an awesome gulf between a God like that and a man like this. It is the tension between a Jacob who desperately clings to his Master: 'I will not let you go except you bless me,' and a Peter, who falls on his face crying, 'Depart from me Lord, for I am a sinful man.'

But the Lord does not depart from people who pray such a prayer. That is news worth sharing.

INDEX OF BIBLICAL REFERENCES